HELPING CHILDREN COPE WITH
ATTENTION DEFICIT DISORDER

DR PATRICIA GILBERT trained at St George's Hospital Medical School, London, and worked in both hospitals and general practice, until specializing in child health. Her work was then mainly in the Community Child Health Service, and she was principal clinical medical officer for South Warwickshire. She was also clinical tutor and visiting senior lecturer in child health at Warwick University for a number of years. She has recently been elected a Fellow of the newly formed Royal College of Paediatrics and Child Health. Writing is now her full-time occupation: a recent publication is a textbook for nursery nurses.

Overcoming Common Problems Series

For a full list of titles please contact
Sheldon Press, Marylebone Road, London NW1 4DU

The Assertiveness Workbook
A plan for busy women
JOANNA GUTMANN

Beating the Comfort Trap
DR WINDY DRYDEN AND JACK
GORDON

Birth Over Thirty Five
SHEILA KITZINGER

Body Language
How to read others' thoughts by their
gestures
ALLAN PEASE

Body Language in Relationships
DAVID COHEN

Calm Down
How to cope with frustration and anger
DR PAUL HAUCK

Cancer – A Family Affair
NEVILLE SHONE

The Candida Diet Book
KAREN BRODY

Caring for Your Elderly Parent
JULIA BURTON-JONES

Cider Vinegar
MARGARET HILLS

Comfort for Depression
JANET HORWOOD

Coping Successfully with Hayfever
DR ROBERT YOUNGSON

Coping Successfully with Migraine
SUE DYSON

Coping Successfully with Pain
NEVILLE SHONE

Coping Successfully with PMS
KAREN EVENNETT

Coping Successfully with Panic Attacks
SHIRLEY TRICKETT

**Coping Successfully with Prostate
Problems**
ROSY REYNOLDS

**Coping Successfully with Irritable
Bladder**
JENNIFER HUNT

**Coping Successfully with Your Hiatus
Hernia**
DR TOM SMITH

**Coping Successfully with Your Irritable
Bowel**
ROSEMARY NICOL

**Coping Successfully with Joint
Replacement**
DR TOM SMITH

Coping with Anxiety and Depression
SHIRLEY TRICKETT

Coping with Blushing
DR ROBERT EDELMANN

Coping with Breast Cancer
DR EADIE HEYDERMAN

Coping with Bronchitis and Emphysema
DR TOM SMITH

Coping with Candida
SHIRLEY TRICKETT

Coping with Chronic Fatigue
TRUDIE CHALDER

Coping with Coeliac Disease
KAREN BRODY

Coping with Cystitis
CAROLINE CLAYTON

Coping with Depression and Elation
DR PATRICK McKEON

Coping with Eczema
DR ROBERT YOUNGSON

Coping with Endometriosis
JO MEARS

Coping with Fibroids
MARY-CLAIRE MASON

Coping with a Hernia
DR DAVID DELVIN

Coping with Psoriasis
PROFESSOR RONALD MARKS

Coping with Rheumatism and Arthritis
DR ROBERT YOUNGSON

Coping with Stammering
DR TRUDY STEWART AND JACKIE
TURNBULL

Coping with Stomach Ulcers
DR TOM SMITH

Overcoming Common Problems Series

Coping with Thyroid Problems
DR JOAN GOMEZ

Coping with Thrush
CAROLINE CLAYTON

Coping with Your Cervical Smear
KAREN EVENNETT

Crunch Points for Couples
JULIA COLE

Curing Arthritis Exercise Book
MARGARET HILLS AND JANET
HORWOOD

Curing Arthritis Diet Book
MARGARET HILLS

Curing Arthritis – The Drug-Free Way
MARGARET HILLS

Curing Arthritis
More ways to a drug-free life
MARGARET HILLS

Depression
DR PAUL HAUCK

Divorce and Separation
Every woman's guide to a new life
ANGELA WILLANS

**Everything Parents Should Know About
Drugs**
SARAH LAWSON

Feverfew
DR STEWART JOHNSON

Gambling – A Family Affair
ANGELA WILLANS

Garlic
KAREN EVENNETT

Good Stress Guide, The
MARY HARTLEY

Heart Attacks – Prevent and Survive
DR TOM SMITH

**Helping Children Cope with Attention
Deficit Disorder**
DR PATRICIA GILBERT

Helping Children Cope with Bullying
SARAH LAWSON

Helping Children Cope with Divorce
ROSEMARY WELLS

Helping Children Cope with Dyslexia
SALLY RAYMOND

Helping Children Cope with Grief
ROSEMARY WELLS

Hold Your Head Up High
DR PAUL HAUCK

How to Be Your Own Best Friend
DR PAUL HAUCK

How to Cope when the Going Gets Tough
DR WINDY DRYDEN AND JACK
GORDON

How to Cope with Anaemia
DR JOAN GOMEZ

How to Cope with Bulimia
DR JOAN GOMEZ

How to Cope with Difficult Parents
DR WINDY DRYDEN AND JACK
GORDON

How to Cope with Difficult People
ALAN HOUEL WITH CHRISTIAN
GODEFROY

**How to Cope with People who Drive you
Crazy**
DR PAUL HAUCK

How to Cope with Splitting Up
VERA PEIFFER

How to Cope with Stress
DR PETER TYRER

How to Enjoy Your Retirement
VICKY MAUD

How to Improve Your Confidence
DR KENNETH HAMBLY

How to Interview and Be Interviewed
MICHELE BROWN AND GYLES
BRANDRETH

How to Keep Your Cholesterol in Check
DR ROBERT POVEY

How to Love and Be Loved
DR PAUL HAUCK

How to Pass Your Driving Test
DONALD RIDLAND

How to Stand up for Yourself
DR PAUL HAUCK

**How to Start a Conversation and Make
Friends**
DON GABOR

How to Stick to a Diet
DEBORAH STEINBERG AND
DR WINDY DRYDEN

How to Stop Worrying
DR FRANK TALLIS

How to Untangle Your Emotional Knots
DR WINDY DRYDEN AND JACK
GORDON

How to Write a Successful CV
JOANNA GUTMANN

Overcoming Common Problems Series

Overcoming Common Problems

Helping Children Cope With Attention Deficit Disorder

Dr Patricia Gilbert

First published in Great Britain in 1998 by
Sheldon Press, SPCK, Holy Trinity Church, Marylebone Road, London NW1 4DU

British Library Cataloguing-in-Publication Data
A catalogue record for this book is available from the British Library

ISBN 0–85969–784–3

Photoset by Deltatype Limited, Birkenhead, Merseyside
Printed in Great Britain by
Biddles Ltd, Guildford and King's Lynn

Contents

Acknowledgements

Thanks are due to the many experts who have written about and discussed this fascinating subject. They have brought to light a hidden disorder which affects a not insubstantial number of children – with possible continuance into adult life.

My personal thanks are also due to the many children with whom I have worked over the years, and to my ever-helpful husband who, once again, has seen me through the complicated minefield of word-processing.

Introduction

Much has been said, and written, over recent years about hyperactive children, and more recently about attention deficit disorder (also called, by some doctors, attention deficit hyperactive disorder – or AD/ HD for short). There is a certain amount of confusion as to what exactly this condition constitutes – and there have been many ways of treating and helping sufferers – and their families.

This book attempts to clarify some of the conflicting descriptions, ideas and treatments of this distressing condition for the benefit of parents and teachers involved with children who suffer from it. A mass of literature on the subject is currently available from all parts of the world – though subsequent work may, of course, overtake some of the conclusions reached. Nevertheless the basic facts regarding the condition will still apply. This text is not meant to be exhaustive, and is not a substitute for advice from, and treatment by, the child's own medical and psychological advisors.

It is hoped that the sufferers themselves – the children – will benefit from a more open discussion of the problems associated with attention deficit disorder and from more consistent handling of their problems. This will enable them to make full use of all available educational facilities in order to attain their full developmental potential.

The child affected by attention deficit disorder is referred to indiscriminately as 'he' or 'she' throughout the book. Although the condition is far more common in boys, this does not exclude a diagnosis of the condition in girls – a possibility which must be recognized in a girl behaving in ways which are typical of the condition.

1

Attention deficit disorder – a general survey

Over the years a wide variety of labels has been attached to children who show excessive hyperactivity. They are said to wear their parents out, disrupt playgroups and nursery classes, and, when school-days begin, they are frequently the children of whom teachers all but despair.

A number of diagnostic labels have also been attached to these children and their symptoms – hyperkinetic syndrome; hyperactivity; over-activity; attention deficit syndrome – and most recently, attention deficit disorder or attention deficit hyperactivity disorder (AD/HD). Attention deficit disorder (ADD) is the general term applied to all subdivisions of this condition, and will be used throughout this book.

There have been marked differences in the past between classifications of this disorder in Britain and America. At the beginning of the 1970s, doctors in Britain were diagnosing very few children as having hyperkinetic syndrome – the term then commonly used in the UK. Less than 0.1 per cent of children were thought to have symptoms of the severe hyperactivity occurring in all situations. The fact is that every child is hyperactive in some way at some time during each day. The common, early-morning cry – 'Let's get up and get on with the day', which disturbs so many parents of children aged from two to five years old – is just one example of normal childhood hyperactivity. Other examples include hyperactivity during special events, or the sheer exuberance while visiting a favourite place or relative. These outbursts of activity are all part of the joy of childhood. Learning to control them appropriately is an important part of the learning process. Most children succeed in doing this during the growing-up years. But children with ADD find this impossible. They are *always* hyperactive, and dash from one activity to another in *every* situation. But in the UK 25 years ago, very few such children were being diagnosed as hyperactive.

By contrast, in the USA in the early 1970s, children with hyperactive behavioural patterns were being diagnosed as suffering from attention deficit syndrome. Relatively large numbers of children – between 5 per cent to 10 per cent of the childhood population – were considered to show the characteristic signs and symptoms. More emphasis was placed, however, on the distractibility and short attention-span of these children than the hyperactivity, which was the basis for diagnosing the hyperkinetic syndrome in the UK.

It almost seemed as if the two countries were looking at two or more different conditions. But recently in Britain, definite criteria have been suggested for the diagnosis of ADD, and the condition is receiving greater recognition. In 1995 it was reported that ADD has been redefined in the *International Classification of Disease* – an international book of classifications of diseases, from which epidemiologists (doctors concerned with disease in large population groups rather than individual patients) gain information on the extent and prevalence of various diseases. In the USA, these criteria – which have been altered over the years – are published in the *Diagnostic and Statistical Manual*; and the current definition is known as DSM–4. Definitions emphasize the difference between hyperactivity and inattentiveness. Specific sub-groups of affected children, who also have other psychological or mental disorders, are also recognized.

Much work has been done – and still is being done – to clarify the confusing situation in many parts of the world. In the 1980s, child psychiatrists in the UK undertook extensive studies to sort out the terminology. In the USA, and in Hong Kong, a mass of research papers has been written on the subject. Experts in New Zealand have queried whether the condition is a product of Western culture. Other reports on ADD are available from such widely diverse places as Turkey, Brazil, Italy, Israel and South Africa. So the problem is evidently not an isolated one! It affects children – and families – on a world-wide basis among the richer nations. ADD is rarely a diagnosis made in developing countries. Other, life-threatening medical problems require more urgent attention.

The first European conference on ADD was held in April 1997 in Oxford. This conference was greatly over-subscribed – which emphasizes the great interest in the condition. A wide variety of professionals – psychiatrists, psychologists, teachers, therapists of all kinds – attended, from most European countries as well as from the USA.

ADD appears to occur more frequently in boys than in girls. This observation may in part be affected by the fact that boys are often seen as being more active and aggressive – although this distinction is becoming less marked nowadays.

In Britain the proportion of children with ADD is generally considered to be between 3 per cent and 5 per cent. This is lower than the US figures – but is nevertheless a marked increase in the previous estimate of 0.1 per cent. From a practical point of view this means that in a class of 30 children, there is probably at least one child with ADD. So it is important that the diagnosis should be made as early as possible – both to help the child and his family, as well as to create a less disturbing environment in the classroom.

ADD has been considered from a variety of angles – chemical, genetic, psychological – some of which have produced positive results (which will be discussed in Chapter 3). Further complications can arise when a child is found to be suffering from another similar condition as well as ADD. This can cause problems, both in diagnosis and treatment. Skilled, knowledgeable help is necessary to sort out these complicated symptoms.

Studies have also shown that ADD can also be recognized in adults. This supports the views that genetic/chemical factors contribute to the disease in children – neither of these factors would alter significantly during a person's lifetime. Strangely enough there does not seem to be a gender difference in adults as in children: men and women appear to be affected in equal numbers.

Summary

So where does all this mass of information available on ADD lead? It leads to the conclusions that:

- around 3 per cent to 5 per cent of children in Britain are probably affected;
- a definite cause has not yet been established;
- early, correct diagnosis is vital;
- the condition can continue into adult life;
- much help can be given to children and their families to minimize the effects of ADD;
- parents, teachers, doctors and social workers should all be involved in giving this help.

2
Signs and symptoms

A good way of defining attention deficit disorder (ADD) can be found in the synopsis of a recent article on the subject: 'The symptoms of attention deficit disorder can cause problems in learning, socialization and behaviour for those individuals affected with it, and put them at high risk of serious psycho-pathology [i.e. psychiatric illness] in adult life' (*Paediatric Nursing* Jan/Feb 1996). These few words set out neatly the wide-ranging effects that can be experienced by both the children themselves and their immediate families. But before looking at ADD, let us consider the part played by learning, socialization and behaviour in a child's development.

The developing child

1 *Learning*
Learning is an integral part of every child's daily life (and probably that of many adults too). Right from Day 1, new-born babies are learning. The shock of emerging into a chilly, bright, noisy world from the relatively warm darkness and silence of the womb is just the first enormous step in the learning process. As the baby grows and matures, she learns many new abilities and skills – how to control her body with all the many actions that developing muscles can perform; how to make sense of the things she sees and hears. In fact, never again do we learn so much in such a short time as during the first two years of life – and all this before formal learning is ever considered. So any problems that affect this learning ability will have a profound influence on every aspect of the child's life.

2 *Socialization*
Socialization also begins in the very early days of life. The first 'social' smile of the four to six week-old baby (as opposed to the windy smile of the first few weeks) is the start of this process. As the months and years pass, children gradually learn acceptable social skills within the context of their cultural background – and these abilities to relate to other people become part of their developing personality. Any

condition – such as ADD, for example – which interferes with this gradual process must have long-term effects on the child's life.

3 Behaviour

Behaviour, too, is all part of the learning and socializing process. Unless the child learns and practises behaviour patterns which fit in which his immediate environment, he will lose many opportunities for socialization and learning.

Continuing problems

The risk of children with ADD suffering psychiatric disorders in later life is perhaps not as certain as the affects of ADD on learning, socialization and behaviour. Nevertheless, it is thought that a percentage of children with ADD will continue to have similar problems in later life. It is hoped that, over the years, ways of handling their disability will emerge so that the typical signs and symptoms of the disorder are less easily recognizable in adults than in children. It is important to remember, however, that help given to the child with ADD can be immensely important in reducing the effects of the condition.

But in order to gain this help, the condition must first be recognized. It is vital that a correct and accurate diagnosis is made before treatment is started.

Symptoms of ADD

The main characteristics of ADD are:

- impulsive behaviour;
- inability to concentrate – or to pay attention – for any length of time;
- excessive hyperactivity;
- boys more frequently affected than girls;
- symptoms all in evidence before the age of seven years;
- symptoms shown continuously for six months or longer.

Without these last two characteristics, a diagnosis other than ADD must be considered.

Let us then look at these main characteristics of ADD in more detail.

Impulsive behaviour

Some of us are naturally more impulsive than others – no sooner thought of, than an action is done for those impulsive ones among us. On the other side of the coin are those super-cautious people who think long and hard over each and every action. This is all part of each individual's unique personality – and every shade of behaviour between these two extremes exists. The child with ADD is right at one end of this personality spread.

Examples of this impulsive behaviour would include the following.

The boy, or girl, who has great difficulty in understanding and following the concept of taking turns. In any nursery game, or task which requires waiting for other children to go first, the child with ADD will push in and insist on being in the lead – whether or not it is appropriate to do so. For example, other children may be better than he is at catching, or throwing, a ball in a team game. Nevertheless, he will insist on doing it – and will probably mess it up in his impulsiveness!

If this behaviour continues over the weeks and months, it will eventually make him unpopular with other children, and so further add to his difficulties.

During a quiet session in the classroom when, for example, a story has been read to a group of children and questions are subsequently being asked about some aspect of the story, the child with ADD will blurt out an answer with little thought as to whether it is right or wrong. This is also an indication of the problems they may have in expressing their thoughts verbally.

Interruptions during the actual reading of the story by ADD sufferers are also typical behaviour in this setting. Again, playmates can become irritated by this, and may shun the child with this type of impulsive behaviour.

Eventually the child with possible ADD becomes so unpopular that he is excluded from other children's games and activities. He will then wander around in the playground intruding on the games and activities of other groups of children. Yet again, this sort of behaviour produces rejection from his peers and irritation in his teachers.

7

More dangerously, the over-impulsive child often reacts physically in an inappropriate way. For example, she may dash across the road with little or no regard for traffic. This is not just bravado – or playing chicken – she just seems unable to stop herself acting on an impulse which tells her to run across the road – now!

Inability to concentrate

Children have to learn the ability to confine themselves to just one task at a time. Normally they learn this gradually and easily, at the same time as they're learning how to run, jump, draw, speak – and acquiring all the other basic everyday skills. When a child discovers a particular interest, she enjoys spending a longer time in investigating and exploring it – from dinosaurs to stamp-collecting. This is not so in children affected with ADD, who might behave in the following ways.

Children with ADD are easily distracted from the interest at hand by any outside noise, sight or even smell. The book or toy is flung down, and the new stimulus investigated – only to be dismissed when some other distraction occurs. This dashing from one task to another interferes greatly with the learning process – especially in children who are old enough to be at nursery or school. An ADD sufferer can never be involved in any activity long enough to learn from it. At home, too, the constant switching from one activity to another becomes very wearing for parents. No sooner is he seated at the table to eat his tea than the child is up to investigate why the dog is barking, or who is walking down the street, for example.

The other side of the coin of the behaviour-pattern just described is that no task is ever completely finished – so even this satisfaction is denied the sufferer. Not for him the pleasure of bringing home from school or nursery a completed picture, but rather an unfinished blob of colour.

A child with ADD rarely listens to the instructions or rules of any game or activity. This is not through any lack of ability to understand what is being explained; rather is it, yet again, the child's inability to listen to any one thing for a long enough time to gain the gist of what is being explained – her concentration is disrupted by ever-present distractions of one sort or another. While other children are able to shut out these potentially distracting aspects of daily living, the child with ADD finds this an impossible task. Her attention is so very easily distracted.

As part of this inability to concentrate, the child with ADD pours forth an almost constant stream of chatter, whether or not this is appropriate, in either its content or its timing. This talk is frequently loud, so that other children's questions, or adult's instructions or requests, are drowned.

We all lose things – sometimes on a daily basis! But the child with ADD is a past master at this. Never does he have the things ready for a planned activity, even though these have carefully been put in his school-bag at the beginning of the day. Somehow they have disappeared or moved to some unlikely place. The child often tries to cover these up by spinning some convoluted yarn of what has happened, who was at fault, or reasons why various articles keep disappearing. So eventually none of his explanations are ever believed – even if they are true.

Excessive hyperactivity

All children are hyperactive when compared with a 70-year-old! All parents, carers and teachers know and expect this, and are usually able to keep up with the children in their care. This can be extremely tiring, but as a child matures, the lively games and tasks are interspersed with quieter, more concentrated, activities. Not so the child with ADD, whose behaviour may be characterized by the following examples.

He has the greatest difficulty in playing quietly – ever. Games and tasks must always be noisy, involving a good deal of loud talk, as well as much running around, long after the age when other children are pursuing quieter activities for significant lengths of time.

Sitting still for longer than a minute or two is absolute anathema to a child with ADD. Even meal-times are periods of constant activity. Even if she can be persuaded to stay sitting in a chair, she will play with plates, cups, salt-cellars, spoons – anything within reach – before moving on to some other activity.

In the nursery or at school, this can be very disturbing for other children, as well as for staff, when, for example, story-time arrives. The ADD sufferer will poke and nudge the other children throughout the quiet time.

As well as showing the above signs of hyperactivity, the child's feet are constantly on the move, his hands will fidget with his hair or clothing, and there will be whole body movements which make one tired just to watch!

For a correct diagnosis of ADD, a child must characteristically behave in at least eight of the ways described above. Other factors, described in the list of symptoms and discussed further below, are also taken into account.

Sex difference

It is known that boys are more often affected with ADD than girls. The figure quoted is that there are three times as many boys as girls with the condition. But just because the sex difference is so marked, it does not mean to say that a girl showing the typical signs and symptoms should be ignored. Looking back in family histories, it can also often be seen that more male members have probably been affected in their childhood than female relatives.

Age

The age at which a child starts to behave in a way characteristic of ADD is also important in establishing the correct diagnosis. All very young babies have a short attention-span. Their nervous systems have not yet matured sufficiently to permit any long periods of concentration. But as children mature, their attention-span on any one activity gradually increases, until, by the age of three to four years old, they will happily pursue an activity in which they are interested for some length of time. Outside distractions also cease to disrupt their concentration much, perhaps causing just a passing glance. This is in direct contrast to the ADD child, who continues to move from toy to toy, being distracted by any outside noise or sight.

The symptoms of ADD should always be evident in three to seven year-olds. Behaviour-patterns such as hyperactivity, impulsiveness or lack of concentration which start in a child who is over seven are not caused by ADD. (See Chapter 4 for other causes which can be confused with attention deficit disorder.)

Duration of symptoms

All children act on impulse – some adults, too – at one time or another. This can be just a personality trait. If the temptation to join in out of turn, or grab a favourite toy, is too great, the impulsive action is taken.

But for most children, this is an isolated incident, and generally out of character. By contrast, the child with ADD is *always* pushing his way to the front of queue, or grabbing a particular toy first – only to discard it a few minutes later, when something else claims his attention. So a further criteria for considering whether or not a child has ADD is that the typical signs and symptoms must have been present continuously for six months or more.

Emma's story

'Why did you push in, Emma? Other children need to play with the rocking horse as well as you, you know. Mrs Tasker was quite cross with you. She said you had been doing this kind of thing for a while.'

Emma and her mother, Penny, were walking home from the playgroup that Emma attended twice a week. Three-year-old Emma's behaviour, both at playgroup and at home, had been giving cause for concern over the past few weeks. From a bright, happy, amicable little girl, Emma was fast becoming the terror of her playgroup – toys were snatched, Emma's voice was constantly heard and it was proving nigh impossible to include her in any group activities.

'I do hope that this behaviour is not going to continue,' Mrs Tasker had said that afternoon. 'Emma does seem to be having problems attending to anything at all of late,' she added.

'Don't care,' Emma pouted in response to her mother's words. 'Can we walk home the long way today?' she added hopefully.

'No not today, Emma – it will soon be Roddy's feed-time. Auntie Sue can only stay to look after him for a little while today. So we had better hurry.'

At this Emma burst into tears and sat down suddenly on the pavement. 'I wish Roddy would go away – I don't like him. Don't want a baby brother!'

Later that evening, after both children were in bed, Penny's thought turned to Mrs Tasker's comments about Emma's lack of attention. Penny had read a little about ADD in a magazine, but had not related it to Emma's recent behaviour. 'Perhaps I had better get some advice,' she thought.

The doctor knew Penny and her children well, and had seen them all through many crises. Having heard the story of Emma's recent altered behaviour, she asked Penny if the problems had started after Roddy's birth – now three months ago.

'Well, yes, I suppose so – yes,' answered Penny. 'Is that why she is being so difficult? I do try to give her more attention when Roddy is asleep, but it's not easy. So it could be that she is just jealous – and not this attention problem thing?'

'You've put it in a nutshell, Penny! Let's try and work out how you can best help Emma to feel that she is still loved and not usurped by Roddy.'

Several weeks later, Mrs Tasker called Penny to one side and said how pleased she was that Emma seemed to have resolved her difficulties. 'She really is her old, happy, helpful self again,' she said.

This situation describes how easy it can be to make a wrong snap diagnosis without looking at all the other surrounding factors which could be affecting a child's behaviour. Penny was fortunate in being given suitable, sensible advice about her daughter's behaviour. The fact that Emma had only been behaving in this way for a relatively short time, that her behaviour had an understandable cause and that it quickly changed once Penny had understood the problem, indicated that she was not suffering from ADD.

Other possible physical signs

Research done in 1971 found a higher-than-expected number of minor physical differences in children who were eventually diagnosed as having ADD. These varied from a single palmar crease (most people have two creases across the palms of their hands), low-set ears and a prominent epicanthus (a specific fold of tissue across the side of the eye next to the nose.)

Not every child with ADD will show all – or indeed any – of these signs, but, if they are present, they can just offer more clues to confirm the diagnosis.

Making a diagnosis

So it can be seen that the criteria for diagnosing ADD are strict. It is important to stress once again that a correct diagnosis must be made. In order for correct, successful treatment to be given, the diagnosis must be certain.

Parents or carers who think that there is a possibility that a child in their care may have ADD should do the following:

12

1   Contact the child's playgroup, nursery or school (depending on the child's age), and establish whether a similar pattern of behaviour has been noticed in these situations as well as at home.
2   Mention the difficulties to the child's own GP. Referral to a paediatrician (a doctor who specializes in the care of children) may well be necessary, as there are a number of other medical conditions that can be confused with ADD. Expert advice from a paediatrician will unravel all the possibilities of the child's behaviour.
3   Appropriate courses of action – at home and at school – can then be taken to reduce the effects of ADD, if this is indeed the eventual diagnosis.

How the parents feel

Having a child with ADD is undoubtedly one of the most physically exhausting situations with which any parent will have to cope. The sheer exhaustion at the end of the day when the affected son or daughter is at last asleep is bad enough. But at this (probably late) hour, feelings of guilt bubble to the surface of the parents' minds. Is it our fault that he is so badly behaved? What have we done wrong? Regrettably, professionals have sometimes answered these, and similar, questions in the affirmative. Parents have been blamed for their child's behaviour – lack of parental discipline and involvement; a working mother; a father absent from home for long periods of time – their inability to care properly for their child being just some of the reasons quoted. And these have been put forward even when there are other children in the same family who have a perfectly normal and acceptable behaviour-pattern.

This attitude adds to the parents' despair. They themselves become further depressed, and less able to cope with the demands of their difficult child. Having, perhaps reluctantly, approached a professional for help, and been told that it is they themselves who need help, does little to raise self-esteem. So as well as feeling guilty, inadequate and exhausted, such parents also do not receive positive help in dealing with their child with ADD.

Matthew's story

Janice and John were delighted when their third baby was a boy. Jemina and Tessa, at five and three years-old respectively, were also happy to welcome their new baby brother, Matthew.

John had a stable job as a long-distance lorry driver. He was often away from home for several days at a time – or even weeks when strikes occurred in Europe. This posed few problems for Janice. She had a part-time job in the evenings which provided her with adult company, as well as some welcome extra cash. Mrs Clarke, a widowed neighbour, was always willing to baby-sit – an ideal set-up which suited everybody. Even with the new baby, Mrs Clarke coped happily with the three children, who were always all ready for bed when Janice left the house.

Problems began, however, when Matt was nearing his second birthday. His energy during the day was something that Janice had never before experienced with her two older children. No afternoon nap for Matthew – he had never wanted one since he was just over a year old. New toys – and his sisters' older toys – were wrecked as soon as he started to play with them. Furniture was no barrier to his undoubted climbing abilities. More than once Janice had had to take him to hospital for treatment for his frequent falls. And when Jemina and Tessa came home from school, tired but happy, the situation became well-nigh impossible. Tea-time had hitherto been a happy, quiet part of the day. Now Matt seemed unable to sit still for even a short while, and his endless stream of chatter interrupted the girl's descriptions of their day at school. Mrs Clarke, too, found her evenings at Janice's house less than happy. 'He doesn't go to sleep until very late, Janice,' she said. 'And he wakes Jem and Tessa by going into their room and sorting through their toys – as well as poking them awake. I don't think I can manage to come for much longer.'

John and Janice discussed the problem during a brief holiday in a caravan during the summer holidays – brief because everyone was finding Matthew's behaviour quite impossible within the restricted space of a caravan. 'Let's go home, John,' Janice said late on the third night of their holiday. She looked exhausted, thin and drawn, with red-rimmed eyes. 'At least Matt's not on top of us all at home. Do you think it is because he is a boy that his behaviour is so awful? We never had this sort of trouble with the girls.'

Having seen the problems that Matthew gave on a daily basis during the holiday, John insisted that they should ask for advice as to how best cope with their son's behaviour. The health visitor was asked to visit. Unfortunately the post had recently been filled by an older woman as a replacement for the health visitor who had helped Janice during the early days with the two girls. After hearing the story of their unfortunate holiday and how Matthew's behaviour had been getting steadily worse, she commented that most of the problems were due to his father's being away from home for such long periods of time. 'A boy needs a father at home as a role-model – and especially in the evenings,' she added, turning to Janice, 'when you are at work.'

Feeling somewhat chastened by her analysis of the situation, Janice and John decided that Janice should give up her evening job – especially as Mrs Clarke had finally decided that she could no longer come to baby-sit. 'I'll try to get home more often in future,' said John, 'but I can't promise. Jobs are hard to come by these days,' he added with a worried frown.

Months passed and, if anything, the situation worsened. Matthew started at a playgroup, but Janice was soon asked to remove him as his disruptive behaviour was upsetting the whole group. Janice was so exhausted and unable to cope that one night she left all three children in the house on their own while she walked the streets trying to think what to do. After this, their case was referred to a social worker.

Fortunately the social worker had had previous experience with a child who had been diagnosed as having ADD. She suspected that this also might be Matthew's problem. She asked for help, through Matthew's GP, from a local paediatrician who was also very much aware of ADD as a condition. Matthew, and his family, were given the treatment necessary to keep his behaviour within acceptable limits. Two years later he has settled in the reception class of a local school, and the whole family once again functions as a happy unit.

Janice and John, in this case study, were fortunate in meeting with someone who had had experience of ADD. Without this piece of good fortune, the situation could have gone from bad to worse, with the possible break-up of the family and certainly a much lowered sense of self-esteem for the parents. They could have been convinced that they were irresponsible parents, and accepted full blame for their son's behaviour – when this was far from the case.

Summary

The signs and symptoms of ADD can be summarized as:

- impulsive behaviour;
- difficulties in concentration;

- hyperactivity;
- boys more frequently affected than girls;
- symptoms are evident in a child below the age of seven years;
- symptoms must be present continually for longer than six months.

3
What causes attention deficit disorder?

The question of what causes attention deficit disorder (ADD) is a difficult one to answer. From the mass of literature on the subject, there are a number of theories as to the causes of ADD. The basic problem seems to be some form of disturbance or dysfunction of the brain, which in turn causes the typical behavioural difficulties seen in the children who are accurately diagnosed as having ADD.

Brain functioning in ADD sufferers

First of all, let us take a brief look at what is thought to be actually happening in the brain (i.e. the neurological aspects) in this condition. In fact, each individual sufferer from ADD probably experiences unique and subtly different aspects of brain development. Different parts of the brain can be affected, and different chemicals can be involved. The particular chemicals thought to contribute to ADD are dopamine, serotonin and norepinephrine – a reduction, or excess, of each of these chemical gives rise to the typical ADD symptoms. Underlying this chemical imbalance is most probably an enzyme defect, which causes either too much or too little of the chemical to be released. (An enzyme is a substance which controls various chemical functions in the body. There are very many enzymes at work in the human body – each with a specific task to fulfil. If just one of these enzymes is absent or faulty, the effects on the chemical control of the body can be far-reaching. Some of the more unusual syndromes and inherited disorders owe all their symptoms and signs to just one vital enzyme being absent or deficient.)

Recent research suggests that the particular symptoms most in evidence in an individual child with ADD depend upon which particular chemical is in imbalance. Following on from this, it is thought that this is also the reason why different types of medication work better for one individual child than another. A child's response to a specific drug will indicate which drug will be of the most value for that individual child. So it may well be necessary for the doctor to prescribe each type of drug in turn, before the most suitable one is found for each individual.

17

Impulsiveness

The impulsive behaviour associated with ADD seems to be related to that part of the brain which inhibits inappropriate behaviour. The chemicals thought to be involved with this type of behaviour are called dopamine and serotonin. The more cautious child considers (maybe only briefly, but nevertheless she does consider) the consequences of her actions and responses to the outside world. Not so the child affected by ADD: he responds with the first thought that comes to his mind. These are the children who rush to answer a question without any consideration as to whether their answer is likely to be right. They, too, are the children who are the most accident-prone – as the following sad event relates.

Thomas's story

The children at the Tots and Toddlers playgroup all had their coats on. They were patiently waiting the arrival of mothers, aunts and friends to pick them up after a happy morning full of interesting, lively activities. Everyone would be glad of lunch and a quiet rest. That is, everyone except Thomas. 'I don't know where he gets his energy from.' sighed Beryl, the playgroup leader, as she grabbed – yet again – the small figure in the bright red anorak who was creating mayhem among the toys which had recently been tidied.

The door opened and a gust of wind made the children gasp. A fall of leaves and a spattering of rain made them all realize that it was still winter. Beryl caught the door as Mrs Wetherby, hands full of shopping and the latest addition to her large family, lumbered into the room. 'It's awful out there,' she puffed, 'and a tree has been blown down over the road. The cars are having to drive on the wrong side of the road over this stretch. Come on, Linda, love. Home-time.' And Mrs Wetherby secured her second youngest in her competent grasp and opened the door again.

A blur of red anorak and flying feet was all that Beryl saw before the screech of brakes and a shout rose above the noise of the wind and rain. 'Thomas! Thomas!' she cried, running out to where the small figure in the red anorak was lying, frighteningly still.

'I couldn't miss him,' the young man bending over Thomas gasped. 'He just ran out straight in front of me.' Beryl knelt down in the wet road and cradled Thomas's head on her knees. 'Where does it hurt, Thomas?' she asked gently. 'My leg – and here,' pointing to his chest. 'Wanted to see the tree . . . wanted . . .' – but the effort was too much

18

for him, and he lapsed into unconsciousness.

Thomas's injuries were severe, and he spent many anxious weeks in hospital before being well enough to return home. His leg had been broken and a small piece of metal had punctured his lung. 'In fact, he's very lucky to be alive,' commented his mother. 'But it doesn't seem to stop him rushing into things,' she added. 'We still have to have our wits about us when Thomas is around – he's still accident-prone.'

Children who behave impulsively, like Thomas, are often termed 'accident-prone'. If there is anything to fall over, they will do so – steps and stairs are a nightmare, as such children's impulsiveness makes them in too much of a hurry to take proper care when negotiating these obstacles. And this accident-proneness can continue into adult life, unless steps are taken early to try and remedy the impulsive behaviour which causes it.

Fortunately Thomas was eventually diagnosed as suffering from ADD. Steps were taken to control his impulsive behaviour, although, as his mother said, everyone in charge of Thomas still had to keep their wits about them.

Lack of concentration

The child whose most obvious difficulties lie in his inability to concentrate has problems in that part of the brain concerned with understanding. This is thought to be caused by a shortage of the chemical dopamine. The child does not process information adequately, so she has difficulty in understanding just what is required of her. This in turn will lead to yet more impulsive behaviour due to misunderstanding, and also to immense frustration because nothing ever seems to work right for the unfortunate child.

Hyperactivity

Children who are exceptionally hyperactive are thought to be suffering from exaggerated responses to normal, everyday situations. The normal processes which restrain and limit responses are unable to cope with this, and so constant activity results. An excessive amount of the chemical norepinephrine is thought to cause this abnormality.

Causes of imbalance in the brain's chemistry

Let us now look at the factors which might be the basic causes of these different forms of brain disturbance. A number of different lines of approach to the problem have been investigated over the years, each of which we shall consider in turn.

Genetic factors

We are all a product of our genes – those minuscule units of DNA passed down to us by our parents at conception, half of our genes coming from our fathers and the other half from our mothers. These are the 'cards' handed out to us at birth; they determine whether we have blue or brown eyes, fair or dark skin; whether we are tall or short, happy or morose – the list is endless. These basic facts are ours for life. Do with them what we will, they can never be altered, only adapted to the environment into which we are born and live.

There is strong evidence that ADD is an inherited condition. A number of studies have confirmed that ADD is more common in children who have a family member (most often a male relative – an uncle or father, for example) who showed symptoms of the condition during their own childhood. In a study of children with ADD, 25 per cent of the biological parents of these children were found to have had a similar behaviour-pattern in their own childhood. By contrast, it was found that children affected by ADD who were adopted had only 4 per cent of their adoptive parents with similar problems in their childhood. Studies have also shown that identical twins (i.e. those who have an identical set of genes, determined at conception) are more likely both to suffer from ADD than are non-identical twins. (Non-identical twins occur when two sperm fertilize two eggs – so each twin's genes are as different as those of any other brother or sister.)

The evidence suggests that genetic factors are largely responsible for ADD. But the environment in which the child is brought up can affect the degree to which the disorder manifests itself. These environmental factors can never cure or entirely remove the symptoms, but can certainly allow the child to live a satisfying, fulfilled life. Equally, an unhelpful environment – where the condition is either not recognized or not handled properly – can worsen the symptoms, and cause much unhappiness for the child and his family. This leads on to other factors which will have a bearing on how well, or otherwise, the child is taught to handle his genetic disorder.

Food allergies

Food intolerance or allergies have received much attention over the years, and have been thought to cause the onset of ADD. In America in the 1970s this theory was especially strong, largely instigated by the work of Dr Ben Feingold. Dr Feingold was a paediatrician specializing in children suffering from such allergic conditions as eczema and asthma. During the course of his work he noticed that, if food containing certain additives and/or aspirin in particular were removed from the child's diet, difficult behaviour patterns improved. He considered this to be especially helpful in dealing with hyperactive children. Feingold Associations were set up in many states in the USA, to give advice on dietary restrictions for hyperactive children. These diets also became popular in the UK and Australia in the late 1970s and early 1980s – but strangely enough were not popular in other parts of Europe or in Scandinavia.

A good deal of scientific research has been done into Dr Feingold's theories on diet and hyperactivity. The results of these studies showed that there was little concrete scientific evidence for any definite link between food additives and hyperactive behaviour. However, some experts believe that certain foods can, in individual children, worsen an existing condition of ADD. Parents and carers closely involved with feeding children on a daily basis are in the best possible position to monitor any link between a specific food and adverse behaviour. So if after eating certain food – chocolate, cheese, yellow-coloured foods containing certain additives, for example – a child's behaviour appears to deteriorate, it is worth excluding these foods for three to four days and noting whether there is any improvement. Alterations to children's diets must, however, be undertaken with care. There are dangers if too many dietary restrictions are applied. It is important to remember the following:

- A full mixed diet is necessary for a child's proper growth and development. Every day, a child must have all the elements of a healthy diet. No attempts must be made to alter a child's diet extensively without the advice of a dietician. She will be able to suggest different foods which will make for a daily balance, and a nutritionally sound diet.
- Too much emphasis on the possibility of a connection between diet and difficult behaviour can blind parents to other possible causes for their child's behaviour – such as those discussed in Chapter 4.
- To keep a child on a restricted diet is time-consuming, often expensive, and can be almost impossible when there is a large family to feed.

- A restricted diet can also cause problems to the child himself. If he cannot eat what all his friends are enjoying, he will feel even more socially isolated. This in itself can give rise to more hyperactivity and anti-social behaviour.
- Food allergy or intolerance plays no part in causing ADD – but it can worsen the behaviour of a child who has been diagnosed as having the condition.

It is worth noting that most foods these days are comprehensively labelled as to their contents. Parents can thus see more readily the exact content of their child's food intake. This is of vital importance for the child who has a proven allergy to a particular food – allergy to peanuts, which seems to be becoming increasingly common these days, is just one example of this.

Remember also that not all food additives are bad: some are vital for preservative functions. Without these substances, bacteria would quickly grow on food-stuffs, and give rise to much illness. Also without them we would have a much more limited range of foods to choose from.

Thyroid abnormality

The thyroid gland is situated in the front of the neck. It is an endocrine gland which affects many body functions. (An endocrine, or ductless, gland is one which secretes hormones directly into the bloodstream, and not through a duct, as is the case with a number of other glands in the body. The effects of the hormones secreted by the ductless glands are far-reaching, and they are extremely rapid in action.)

An over-active thyroid gland causes all the body's mechanisms to speed up, and can frequently give rise to over-activity. Children can sometimes be affected by over-activity of this gland, and their ensuing behaviour can be very similar to that of a child with ADD. However, no relationship at all has been found between the two disorders – though it is important that a malfunctioning thyroid gland is eliminated as a cause for an individual child's hyperactivity.

Other possible factors in causing ADD

Malnutrition

Early childhood malnutrition has been put forward as a possible factor in causing ADD. Malnutrition, as well as being due to parenting difficulties and social problems, can also be caused by other diseases which prevent the food from being properly processed or absorbed. Coeliac disease, in which there is an allergy to gluten (the protein found in wheat and wheat-foods), is one example of this.

Alcohol abuse

Alcohol abuse by the mother during her pregnancy has also been suggested as being a contributory factor to ADD. If this abuse has been so severe that the baby is born with a low birth-weight and/or possible mental retardation, the chances are higher that he will also be affected by ADD.

Lead poisoning

Lead poisoning has been suggested as a potential factor in the development of ADD. There is, however, little evidence to suggest that this is the case. Blood lead-levels are not found to be consistently high in children affected with ADD.

Smoking

Smoking by the mother during pregnancy has been investigated as a possible factor in causing subsequent ADD in children. Research in the USA has shown that 22 per cent of children diagnosed as having ADD had mothers who smoked during their pregnancy; by contrast, only 8 per cent of children without ADD had mothers that smoked during their pregnancies. So while it cannot be categorically stated that smoking causes ADD, there is a strong enough link to make it advisable for mothers-to-be to give up smoking.

It has been found that adolescent children with ADD are more likely to smoke than their peers who don't have the condition. They also find it extremely difficult to kick the habit. Maybe they started smoking in an attempt to manage their inability to concentrate, or in an attempt to improve their social skills.

Association of ADD with other syndromes

There appears to be a greater than expected number of children with ADD who also have a further condition or syndrome. Three such conditions have been identified:

- Sufferers from Tourette syndrome are also sometimes affected by ADD. Tourette syndrome is a condition in which the child has physical tics – such as constant shrugging of shoulders or blinking – along with involuntary shouting of rude words at inappropriate times. Hyperactivity can also be a symptom of this syndrome. Both children and adults can be affected by Tourette syndrome – although adults can learn to control the symptoms to some extent. There is no actual proven link between the two conditions – it is just that ADD occurs more frequently if the child also suffers from Tourette syndrome.

- Neurofibromotosis sufferers have similarly been found to have an associated diagnosis of ADD. Sufferers from this condition – both children and adults – have non-cancerous swellings in various parts of the body. They may also have many *café-au-lait* (coffee-coloured) spots all over the body. Problems can arise when the swellings become so large as to press on, and affect the function of, various vital organs of the body. Again, there is no proven link between ADD and this condition – but the two conditions sometimes occur together.
- Phenylketonuria is a condition, caused by the absence of a vital enzyme, in which the body is unable to handle the essential amino acid, phenyl-alanine. A number of everyday foods (such as meat, fish, cheese and eggs) have a high phenyl-alanine content. Vegetables such as peas and beans are also high in this substance, so the sufferer's diet is very restricted. For some as-yet-unknown reason, such a diet seems to put a child at greater risk of suffering from ADD.

Summary

- There are strong possibilities that attention deficit disorder is a genetically inherited condition;
- Food allergies play no part in causing the condition, but certain foods can worsen an existing problem;
- Thyroid abnormality is in no way linked with ADD;
- Smoking during pregnancy may have some bearing on the subsequent onset of the condition;
- Alcohol abuse during pregnancy can be a potential causative factor;
- Early childhood malnutrition may have a bearing on the onset of ADD;

- Lead poisoning has been investigated, and is not thought to be a factor;
- There is a strong link between ADD and certain other syndromes or conditions.

4

Other reasons for difficult behaviour

As has already been stressed, it is vital that a correct diagnosis is made before any attempts are made to help the child, and his family, to cope with his difficult behaviour. There are a number of conditions which can mimic attention deficit disorder (ADD) – and which can, at times, exist alongside ADD, making the child's problems even more difficult to unravel.

Before ADD is firmly diagnosed, a number of other medical and/or psychological conditions must be excluded and, of course, receive appropriate treatment if they are found. It is important that the child with difficult behaviour is medically examined, at the very beginning of investigations. It is tragic indeed if a child with a treatable medical condition – such as deafness, for example – were to be labelled as having ADD, while the physical cause of his problems remained unrecognized.

These other possible reasons for difficult behaviour in children can be broadly divided into two categories – physical and psychological reasons. There can be a certain amount of overlap between these conditions, as well as between them and ADD.

Physical conditions

Deafness

Deafness is a relatively common condition is early childhood. Upper respiratory tract infections (such as colds or tonsillitis) are common-place, as the child's immunity to various infections is being built up – and the middle ear is frequently involved in these infections, sometimes resulting in fluctuating deafness. This type of deafness can be especially difficult to pin-point, as it varies in degree from day to day, sometimes hearing being excellent and at other times poor. This can last for many weeks after the infection has cleared. It is caused by sticky mucus from the infection remaining in the middle ear. (It is a well-known fact that a child with a fluctuating deafness will have perfect hearing on the day that hearing-tests are held at the school!)

The effect of this fluctuating condition on a child can be very marked. For example, she may well hear only half of what her mother or teacher is asking her to do – and as a result may do exactly the opposite to what has been asked of her. She will not then be able to understand why she is being blamed for doing what she thought was wanted. If this happens with monotonous regularity, she will become irritated and frustrated at this – to her – puzzling behaviour of adults. Difficult behaviour can then become more pronounced as the result of her confusion; impulsive behaviour and hyperactivity could well be her way of dealing with these problems.

Children who have frequent upper respiratory tract infections should be carefully checked for hearing-loss, once the infection has cleared. This should be done on a number of separate occasions, to allow for the possibility of fluctuating deafness.

Special care must also be taken with children who have frequent courses of antibiotics for middle-ear infections. The condition, 'glue ear' – in which the tiny bones in the middle ear become unable to move adequately due to sticky mucus – can be the result of this (necessary) treatment, and can again cause fluctuating deafness. Anti-congestant medicines, or, in severe cases, a myringotomy (in which the ear-drum is pierced and the sticky fluid removed under a general anaesthetic), can be necessary to cure glue ear. Some children, however, do not need such treatment: normal growth of the nasal and ear passages allows the sticky secretions to drain away.

A further type of deafness, called sensori-neural deafness, involves damage to the actual nerves of hearing. This condition can be present from birth, or may occur as the result of a viral infection – for example, following an attack of measles or meningitis. Special teaching methods are often necessary for children with this severe form of deafness. Again, if this type of deafness passes unnoticed – and, with the emphasis on screening for such conditions for all babies in Britain, it is hoped that it will always be diagnosed – behavioural problems can result.

The concerns of parents regarding their child's hearing must always be listened to. If a child's mother says he is deaf, he probably *is* deaf!

Visual difficulties

Every child's vision should be tested at regular intervals – but changes in visual acuteness can alter rapidly between these check-ups. Between the ages of 27 months and four-and-a-half years-old (the ages at which routine eye-tests are usually done), a child's vision can change from normal to short-sighted. This means that distant objects appear to be very blurred.

Young children are unable to explain that they can't see properly. So part of what they are being shown can easily be misunderstood (just as a deaf child misunderstands sounds). This in turn can lead to seemingly difficult, disobedient behaviour, because the child has misunderstood what is meant. So, in any consistent behavioural problem, an eye-test should be done – especially so for a child who has only recently started to have behavioural difficulties.

Petit mal

Petit mal is a further medical condition which must be excluded in a child with behaviour problems, before ADD can be firmly diagnosed. *Petit mal* is a particular form of epilepsy in which the sufferer 'switches off' for a few seconds: she will stop talking in mid-sentence, or stop working at a task for a short while; her eyes will stare blankly into space, while an abnormal electrical discharge passes through the brain. Then the conversation is picked up again, or the activity resumed, as if there had been no break. Children who suffer from these 'absences' (another common term used for *petit mal*) are often thought to be day-dreaming. So while quiet, introspective children do day-dream at times, if this is a frequent occurrence, and there is also a falling-off of performance at school, the possibility of *petit mal* must be excluded by referral to a paediatrician.

Absences can occur at frequent intervals throughout the day, so over the course of a few hours the child may miss a good deal of what has been going on around her. So, once again, she can appear to be difficult, or disobedient, if she only registers a small part of what is expected of her.

Petit mal can be treated very successfully with a specific drug, so medical advice should be sought if playgroup leaders, nursery nurses or teachers – as well as parents – have a persistent day-dreamer in their charge.

Learning difficulties

Learning difficulties can also manifest themselves in bad behaviour. The child who finds it difficult to do things which his peers seem to find easy will often create a disturbance in an attempt to hide his disabilities. Frustration at not being able to join in successfully with games, because of lack of understanding, can also lead to outbursts of anger.

If there are suspicions that a learning difficulty – perhaps only in one specific area of development, such as speech, movement or memory, for example – may be present, a multi-disciplinary assessment is necessary. Referral to a child development centre through a health visitor, GP or paediatrician will ensure that the child's strengths and weaknesses are thoroughly sorted out. Any problem in one specific area can then be given special attention. When the child is taught at a level appropriate to his own particular needs, his behaviour will improve.

In the school situation, the special needs advisor can help in sorting out the right educational needs for each individual child.

A child may, of course, have learning difficulty as well as suffering from ADD – and the signs and symptoms of each condition can be difficult to unravel. It is, however, essential to try to do so, in order that both conditions can be appropriately treated. It is thought that around 20 per cent of children with ADD may also have some other conditions as well.

ADD itself may also be the basic cause of learning problems. The child's inattention and lack of concentration resulting from his ADD will not help his learning abilities.

Specific syndromes

There are a number of specific syndromes which can closely mimic ADD. (A syndrome is a specific mixture of physical symptoms which together make up a specific condition – it is frequently an inherited condition.) One of the commonest syndromes to be confused with ADD is Tourette's syndrome. This syndrome is characterized by:

- frequent physical tics, ranging from repetitive whole-body movements, to twitching of the face, hands or eyes;
- vocal tics in which the affected child involuntarily shouts out a variety of, usually obscene, words or phrases and swear-words.

The constant hyperactivity of the body can be very reminiscent of ADD.

Other rare syndromes and disorders – such as Fragile X syndrome (a recently recognized inherited condition, its main features being: learning difficulties, speech problems, and a long, thin face) or over-activity of the thyroid gland (described briefly in Chapter 3) – can also be confused with ADD and expert medical advice is needed to sort them out.

Side-effects of drugs

Certain drugs, given for some condition such as epilepsy or asthma, can have side-effects causing behavioural changes similar to those seen in a child affected by ADD. Again, it is important that this unwanted side-effect should be identified and, if possible, a change of medication offered.

Conduct disorders

Other conduct disorders and emotional–behavioural disorders will also have to be excluded, with psychiatric help, before ADD can be firmly diagnosed.

A child with a conduct disorder shows very obvious antisocial tendencies. His behaviour is aggressive, he may steal, treat animals cruelly and, at worse, commit arson and vandalize property. EBD – emotionally and behaviourally disturbed – children can also exhibit a wide variety of behavioural problems. They have a low self-esteem, are often anxious or depressed, relate badly to their peers and are often sullen and unco-operative.

Child abuse

Child abuse must, sadly, always be remembered as a possible cause for difficult behaviour. Abuse can take a number of different forms:

- physical abuse;
- sexual abuse;
- neglect;
- emotional abuse.

The first three of these forms of abuse will have probably more definite and obvious signs and symptoms than emotional abuse. Briefly, physical abuse results in bruising, and even fractures, for which no good explanation is given. Sexual abuse will give rise to possible urinary tract infections, fear of the opposite sex or precocious sexual knowledge. Neglect will be evident by loss of weight, lack of cleanliness in both body and clothing.

Emotional abuse can manifest itself in a child's difficult behaviour. The child who is always shouted down at home, told she is useless, and has no one to take any interest in her activities, for example, can respond in one of two different ways. She will either go along with the messages given to her at home, and lack in any self-esteem, or she will assert herself in no uncertain manner outside the home situation. This may result in hyperactive, disobedient or noisy disruptive behaviour.

Distinguishing behaviour caused by emotional abuse from that of a child with true ADD is difficult. Much careful detective work from all the disciplines concerned with the welfare of the child is necessary. It may be that a case conference is called, at which the parents also provide an input. Parents who find their role difficult may, at times, be quite unaware of the effect their attitudes are having on their child.

The presence of ADD itself can, of course, make the child more liable to abuse. Parents who would cope perfectly adequately with usual high spirits, find the behaviour-patterns of a hyperactive child just too much for them – and this can result in some form of abuse.

Psychological conditions

Psychological conditions are more tenuous, but can often give rise to behavioural problems for a limited time-span. These can be distinguished from ADD by the relative shortness of time over which the child's behaviour has been difficult. (Remember that one of the important criteria for diagnosing ADD is that the difficulties must have been present for at least six consecutive months).

Home circumstances

Children from homes where guidelines for behaviour are lax or non-existent, where discipline is poor, or whether there is little love and/or interest taken in them, will often try to compensate for this by their attention-seeking behaviour outside the home. This can take the form of butting in on other children's games, offering toys or sweets in order to gain popularity, or other ways of gaining the attention they otherwise lack.

The whole family needs help in these difficult circumstances. The child's behaviour is just one facet of a whole family which is not working as it should.

Even a less difficult situation – such as a family where decision-making is haphazard or quarrelsome – can affect the children's behaviour badly. Parents must present a united front when dealing with their children – even if they disagree later, in private! Children get very confused over getting different 'messages' from each parent – and they can become very adept at playing off one adult against another. Grandparents who are too closely involved in the day-to-day dynamics of the family where there are young children can, at times, lead to problems. Lines of communications between parents and children need to be clear-cut.

The child who is affected by ADD will have yet further difficulties under these circumstances.

Unsettling events

Other specific upsets in a child home-life can cause temporary behaviour problems. These can be confused with ADD, unless the strict diagnostic criteria are remembered. Such upsets can include:

- the arrival of a new baby. Feelings of jealousy can produce difficult behaviour outside the immediate surroundings of home. However, with parental sensitivity and a little extra attention at the nursery or school, these problems will soon be resolved.
- Moving house can also upset some children – especially if the move is closely followed by the arrival of another child in the family. The child's world has seemingly been turned upside-down, and there seem to be just too many things with which to cope. Again, a little extra attention and some careful explanation and reassurance are probably all that is needed.
- Separation or divorce are now recognized as having a far greater effect on the children involved than was hitherto thought to be the case. The age of the child when the family breaks up may be important: around three years old seems to be the worst time for adverse effects. Today's marriages frequently break up within the first 10 years, and this means that, more often than not, there are young children involved. And even if there is a successful re-marriage, there may still be problems with step-brothers and sisters to be overcome. All this may produce bad behaviour in a child.
- Bereavement – perhaps in the form of the death of a much-loved grandparent – can upset a child's equilibrium. Again, if this occurs when the child is around three years old, this seems to be the most vulnerable time. The most usual reaction is probably for the child to become quiet and withdrawn, but at times feelings of anger – even against the surviving grandparent – can burst out.

Position in the family

Does the position of the child in the family have any bearing on behaviour? There is no doubt that children of different family ranking do get treated differently by their parents. The first child receives all his parents' love and attention – and also all their inner anxieties as to their capabilities as parents! This first child also bears the brunt of adjustment to the arrival of younger brothers or sisters. If he remains an only child, he may feel that he has to try especially hard to live up to the expectations of his parents.

It is often said that it is the middle child of three who presents the most difficult behaviour. She is neither expected to be the most responsible child (this is the burden of the eldest), nor yet is she the youngest for whom more allowances are made.

Summary

All these different factors can give rise to difficult behaviour of one kind or another, for varying lengths of time. Unless all the characteristics of ADD are remembered, bad behaviour caused by any one of these many factors can be confused with true ADD – and this means that children and families will not get appropriate help.

So ADD can be confused with:

- physical conditions, such as deafness, visual problems, *petit mal*;
- learning difficulties and other syndromes;
- the effects of child abuse;
- the effects of family life, or of other temporary upsets in day-to-day living.

5

Coping with attention deficit disorder

There is much evidence to show that attention deficit disorder (ADD) is a definite clinical condition caused by specific chemical imbalances. There is no actual brain abnormality – but there appears to be a deficiency in the way in which messages in the brain are transmitted. As we have seen, there are a number of other conditions which can closely resemble ADD, and care must be taken to exclude these other causes of problematic behaviour. They, too, will need specific treatment – often quite different from that necessary to help the child with ADD.

It is vital that ADD is recognized as early as possible, both from the child's and the parent's viewpoint.

From the parent's point of view, life with a child suffering from ADD is a nightmare. Friends and colleagues – and certainly strangers, in the supermarket, for example – can provoke feelings of guilt and worry as to whether their child's behaviour is their fault. Friendships can be lost, and even other family members may hesitate to include these relatives in their activities. Celebrations – such as birthdays or Christmas, for example – can be lonely if no one invites the family with an ADD sufferer. Alternatively, the occasion can become a disaster if the family is invited and the difficult child is at his very worst. These aspects, added to the inevitable exhaustion and worry of meeting the child's day-to-day needs, make the lot of the parent of a child with ADD an unenviable one.

From the child's point of view, her self-esteem diminishes weekly as yet more friends shun her. She is seldom, if ever, invited home to play with other children – and if she is, and it probably only happens once! In an attempt to gain attention, her behaviour becomes even worse. These secondary behavioural problems pose more difficulties in controlling behaviour.

The people who cope

So, early recognition of ADD is vital for everyone concerned – and for a successful outcome in dealing with the disorder. Once the diagnosis has been established, much can be done to help both the child and other

34

family members. A multi-disciplinary approach must be used, a
fully correlated to obtain full benefit. Four main groups of people will
need to become involved: parents, medical staff, teachers and social
workers.

Parents

Parents obviously play a major role in caring for the ADD sufferer –
especially in the day-to-day, routine help needed by their son or
daughter. Initially, they have to recognize and think through their
attitudes to their son or daughter. Perhaps they need help – and/or
permission – to lead a life of their own, with their own interests. They
must not become completely weighed down by their child's difficulties and behaviour (see Chapter 6).

Medical staff

A medical input is needed, both from GPs and psychiatrists,
particularly in the early stages, in order to diagnose the condition and
to set out lines of treatment. Possible drug treatment may be
prescribed, and parents will need ongoing help in monitoring the
effects of such treatment. Parental worries about long-term drug
treatment will also need to be addressed.

Health visitors – who are often knowledgeable about, and intimately
concerned with, the dynamics of the families they visit – are also
extremely valuable in giving regular help. A health visitor may well be
the first person to identify a severe, or unusual, behaviour problem.
With her knowledge of the family, perhaps over many years, she will
be able to say, with a fair degree of certainty, that the type of behaviour
is unusual for this particular family.

Teachers

Teachers at nursery or school play a vital part in the treatment of the
child with ADD. As children mature, they spend more and more time
away from home, and in the care of teaching staff of one kind or
another. So once again, it is vital that teachers are familiar with the
condition, and that they understand the basic principles behind
treatment. They must also be familiar with the procedures for referral
to other professionals, who can provide specialized help for each
individual child. For example, educational and clinical psychologists
have many skills in dealing with difficult children, and it is important
that every avenue should be explored to help the child and his family.

also need to be involved in the care of an ADD sufferer. ent may come at an early stage, following a complaint up or nursery about a particular child who is showing bad behaviour. They can offer considerable help, especially in liaising between home and school or nursery.

Each of these groups of people has a specific part to play in the care of the child with ADD. It is important that good communication is established between everyone involved – lines of communication can so easily become crossed, making for less than perfect treatment for the child. Remember, too, that the child himself will quickly pick up discrepancies in his treatment – and exploit them. There is nothing wrong with his intelligence! If possible, parents, teachers, social workers and health visitors should meet occasionally, to pool their knowledge of the child's progress and work out further strategies together.

Explaining to the child

The child affected with ADD needs an explanation of her condition, and why she is apparently being treated differently from her peers:

- Why should she have to take medicine?
- Why should she have certain tasks to do at home or at school?
- Why do special arrangements have to be made for her?. Why shouldn't her brothers and sisters have to do the same?

These may be just some of the questions asked – or perhaps worried about internally and not verbalized.

To explain ADD to a child is not an easy task, and maybe parents are not the best people to undertake it. Remember that they have been at the sharp end of their child's behaviour – perhaps for a long time. Tempers will understandably have become frayed at one time or another, and this is not the best situation for giving – or receiving – information. Perhaps the health visitor or social worker would be the best person to talk to the child, listening to his worries, and answering his very natural questions about his situation. Or maybe some other person, more remote from day-to-day events, could undertake the task. A knowledgeable (that is important) and favourite aunt or uncle, for example, may be a possibility.

Obviously, explanations must be geared to the child's age and ability to understand. But it is important that his reasonable queries should be answered calmly and honestly. Fear of the unknown affects us all, and this is probably even more true for the child with ADD. He may find it very difficult to understand why he is so unpopular, and why he is having to be treated differently from his play-fellows.

Children affected by ADD should preferably be offered help in their own homes and in their local nursery or school, if at all possible. Occasionally, however, the local situation may have deteriorated so drastically tht the child may have to live away from home for a period of time. Residential schooling in Britain is becoming a less common option than it was a decade or so ago. Special units at local schools are available in many areas of the country to deal with special problems. But still it is occasionally necessary for a child to spend a few months staying at a special school. For this to happen, the child has to be 'statemented'. This is a procedure initiated by the local education authority, which involves medical staff, educational psychologists and social workers in assessing the best facilities for each individual child. But before this stage is reached, certain actions and steps must be taken by the school. (See Chapter 7 for procedural steps and benefits of the statementing procedure.)

Effects on other children

The effect on other children in the family must also not be forgotten or ignored. As with any handicapping condition (and ADD *is* a handicapping condition), the whole family is involved. Embarrassment at, and affection for, the affected brother or sister will both be expressed by other children in the family. Loyalty to their brother or sister may prevent them from making friendships – it can be highly embarrassing to bring a friend home to a house where shouting matches, disruptive behaviour and general hyperactivity are commonplace. Parents, too, may have become so involved with their child with ADD that attention to the other children's needs is pushed into second place – not by any deliberate act, but by sheer lack of time and energy.

Tom's story

'Jeremy wants me to play at his house today, Mum,' stated Tristan, dumping his school bag on the kitchen table. 'Is that alright?'

'Yes, of course, dear,' replied Susie Tuck. 'But do ask Jeremy round here sometimes,' she added to her son's retreating back. At this moment an almighty crash resounded through the house, followed by a loud scream. Susie hurried upstairs to where sounds of battle were obvious. Opening the door of nine-year-old Jessica's room, a scene of disaster met her eyes. Books, papers, tapes and Jess's beloved chess set were scattered all over the floor – and in the middle lay a smashed portable TV set.

'Tom did it, Mum,' cried Jess. 'He came in and wanted to turn on the TV. I told him not to, because I was reading and listening to . . .' Tears got the better of Jess's limited control, and she rushed into her mother's arms.

'It's all right, love. It can be mended,' soothed Susie, looking around the room for signs of the culprit who had wrought this havoc. 'He's under my bed,' whispered Jess, aware that her mother was looking for her younger brother, Tom.

Tom had recently been diagnosed as having ADD. Treatment had been arranged, and a few successes were being noticed, but in the late afternoon and early evening things were still volatile. Susie put this down to the effects of the lunch-time dose of the medicine wearing off.

'I do wish Tom would get better quicker,' Jessica confided to her mother later that evening, when Tom was at last asleep. 'We could have our friends round then, and maybe they could stay the night. Oh, sorry, I shouldn't have said that. Tristan told me not to. We do love Tom, but he is such a menace. We didn't want to hurt your feelings . . . Oh dear, I am getting in a muddle.'

At the weekend Susie was sitting in the garden with Tristan and Jessica. The children's father, Guy, had taken Tom swimming, and all was peace. 'Is it Tom that stops you asking your friends home?' asked Susie quietly. Jess and Tristan exchanged glances. After a moment's silence Tristan spoke, 'Well, yes. You see, everyone else's small brothers play quietly on their own or with their own friends. And . . . and,' Tristan swallowed nervously, 'they all say they don't want to come here if Tom's here. So we don't ask them any more,' he added quietly.

Later that evening, Susie and Guy were discussing the earlier conversation with the two older children. 'We've been concentrating too much on Tom's problems,' Guy said firmly. 'I don't know about you, Susie, but I didn't realize the effect all this was having on Tristan and Jessica.' Susie nodded her agreement. 'We must try and give them a bit more of our time and attention. Thank goodness Tom's behaviour is a bit better these last few days – so perhaps life will get easier soon.'

These events illustrate the involvement of a whole family when one member has a disabling condition. It can be all too easy for parents to concentrate their whole attention on the most obvious problem – in the above case, Tom – and virtually to ignore the needs of other children.

A cure for ADD?

Finally it must be remembered that there is no definite permanent 'cure' for ADD. Help, in many forms, can be given to enable sufferers to learn to live with their condition, and to alleviate the social, relationship and educational difficulties which arise from the behavioural patterns connected with ADD. Consequently, treatment needs to be lifelong. But as the child matures and learns various techniques for adjusting to his disorder, these gradually become more and more a part of his everyday, normal behaviour. These coping techniques, learned in childhood, may well account for the much smaller number of adults with ADD symptoms.

Summary

- ADD must ideally be recognized early;
- a multi-disciplinary approach is necessary for treatment;
- parents need help as well as the child;
- affected children need a thorough explanation;
- the effect on other children in the family must not be forgotten;
- the correct place for treatment must be assessed;
- treatment needs to be lifelong.

6

How to cope at home

By the time attention deficit disorder (ADD) has been fully and accurately diagnosed in a child, his parents will probably be near the end of their abilities to cope with his behaviour. Their whole life will seem to be spent in avoiding embarrassing situations, and in trying to find some way of keeping their child happy and occupied for longer than a few minutes at a time. Help for both parents and child is urgently needed.

It is important to realize from the outset that this help must involve a wide range of carers from the two situations in which the child spends most of his life – home, and either nursery or school. So parents, teachers, nursery nurses, psychiatrist, psychologist, paediatrician, health visitor and social worker must be involved at some time or other in the child's day-to-day life. Lines of communication must also be first-class between all the people involved in the care of each individual child. It is useless for a certain behaviour-plan to be followed conscientiously at home when entirely different behaviour-patterns are expected at school, for example. As well as confusing the child – with the probable result that his behaviour will further deteriorate – such a situation will allow him to manipulate the people involved. Remember that he is not stupid, and can well take advantage of the different ways of handling his behaviour.

As mentioned in Chapter 5, it is a good idea, if possible, for everyone involved in the child's care to meet at regular – even if infrequent – intervals to assess progress and plan the future. This is not always practical, but at least parents and teachers (or nursery staff) should be in regular weekly, if not daily, contact. Successes, and failures, can then be discussed. Perhaps a slightly different approach to a specific problem can be sorted out informally at these regular exchanges of information.

Treatment and care of the boy or girl with ADD is based on a three-pronged approach:

- counselling;
- behaviour modification;
- medication.

For the greatest success all three methods must be used, and co-ordinated. In this chapter, we shall consider the first two methods; medication is covered in Chapter 8.

Counselling

The parents of an affected child, by the relatively late stage at which a definite diagnosis has been established, will need:

- help in understanding what is causing their child's difficult behaviour;
- to be able to look at, and come to terms with, their own attitudes to their child;
- to know about what can be done to help;
- help in understanding fully that treatment is, of necessity, long-term;
- support to restore their own, probably battered, self-esteem.

Understanding ADD

The very first thing that parents need is a face-to-face explanation of what is causing their child's bad behaviour. The paediatrician involved in making the diagnosis is the best person to give these explanations. He or she will be able to explain fully the way in which the diagnosis has been reached; the steps which have been taken to exclude the other possible causes for the child's behaviour-patterns; the fact that it is not the parents' fault that their child has ADD; and, most important of all, that something can be done.

Following this initial explanation, parents usually feel enormously relieved – but probably also slightly bemused at the whole situation. Follow-up, with written material on ADD, is necessary, together with referral to someone with an intimate knowledge of the condition who can answer the inevitable questions which will arise over the succeeding weeks. Anyone visiting a doctor with any condition usually only recalls a small percentage of what has been explained. Further explanations are often needed – either at a later visit, or in written material, or by someone else at a later date. With a complex condition such as ADD this is especially true. On subsequent visits, it is a good idea for parents to write down a list of questions to ask – and probably to jot down the answers as well.

As far as written material is concerned, the literature from the ADD Family Support Group UK is invaluable (their details are listed under

Useful Addresses). Health visitors and GPs who have a particular interest in the condition can also be very helpful in clearing up problems and misunderstandings.

Parental attitudes

The parents' attitudes to their affected child are also important, and need to be brought to the surface and examined. For example, are the parents:

1 embarrassed by their child?
2 frightened of their child?
3 disappointed in their child? or
4 do they just regard him as a nuisance?

1 Embarrassment

Embarrassment at a consistently badly-behaved child is all too easy to understand. Rightly or wrongly we all tend to think of our children as an extension of ourselves rather than as people in their own right. This is inevitable in the very early days of life, when a baby is totally dependent. But as she matures and develops her own personality, evidence accumulates – fast! – that she really is a separate, and individual, person. Parents must provide guidelines as to acceptable behaviour, and moral understanding, throughout the years of child-hood and adolescence – but in adult life she is noticeably quite a different person from her parents. Certain characteristics may be similar – but quite differently expressed and used.

Remember, too, that the child with ADD has a disability. He did not choose to be impulsive, lack concentration or be hyperactive – these were the genes he inherited. Parents should be helped to understand that in no way is this their fault – they need not be concerned that ADD is most probably an inherited disorder, any more than if their child were suffering from asthma, Down's syndrome, or any other of the multitude of conditions that can be handed down the generations.

2 Fear

Some children with ADD can be truly frightening – particularly as they get older. Their behaviour is such that parents wonder whatever will happen next – a physical assault on themselves or some other person, or yet a further accident to an accident-prone, impulsive child. Again, this is an eminently understandable reaction – especially if the typical behaviour has been going on for some time. Parents can become completely discouraged, and be utterly at a loss as to how to control their wayward child. Parents who have reached this unhappy state need a lot of help – help in understanding themselves and their reactions to their child's behaviour, and also in understanding what is actually happening to the child himself. Once treatment has started the situation should improve, and once again affection for, rather than fear of, their son or daughter will be uppermost.

Bobby's story

Grandma Farley was over 70, and arthritic, when she came to live with Bill and Lesley. Lesley was fond of her mother. She was looking forward to helping her with the daily chores and shopping, which her mother now found difficult.

'The only thing that bothers me about Mum being here, Bill,' Lesley said one evening when Mrs Farley had retired to bed, 'is the way Bobby behaves towards his Gran. The other day I heard him swearing at her and saw him kicking at her table. I think Mum's a bit frightened of him – I am, too, at times,' she added, under her breath.

Bobby, now six years old, had arrived as an afterthought to the couple whose two elder children were away from home, at work and at college. Since the early days, Bobby had been a difficult child – quite unlike Tim and Judy, the two older children. Lesley had thought that school would, as she put it, 'tame' Bobby. But exactly the opposite seemed to be happening. He was becoming even more impulsive and hyperactive. Lesley, now in her mid-forties, was finding it increasingly difficult to control his behaviour.

'You're just feeling a bit run down, old thing,' Bill looked at his wife over the evening paper. 'You can't be frightened of a six-year-old!'

'But I am, Bill,' admitted Lesley. 'Just listen to him upstairs now! He should have been asleep hours ago, but it sounds as if he's still jumping around. And if I go up, he'll probably throw something at me.' Lesley sighed, and surreptitiously wiped away a tear. Bill put down the paper. 'You really are scared aren't you, Lesley? Make an appointment to see Dr Horley as soon as possible. Perhaps you need a tonic.'

On his way to work the following morning, Bill mulled over the events of the previous evening. 'The other children didn't give Les these sort of problems,' he thought, 'Perhaps it's her age? And all the extra work Grandma is making?' Meanwhile Lesley was sitting in the waiting room at the doctor's surgery. She had finally got Bobby off to school with all the extras he needed for the day – and which he always seemed to forget. 'I'll sit and wait until Dr Horley is free,' she had said to the receptionist. 'I need to see her today.'

An hour and a half later, Lesley walked into the consulting room. Dr Horley listened closely to Lesley's description of her feelings about her young son, and his behaviour to her and his grandmother. 'And we are having complaints about his behaviour at school, too,' Lesley said tearfully. 'I feel at a complete loss as to how to cope with Bobby – and I'm really frightened that he'll hurt his Grandma one day. He actually kicked her yesterday. I didn't dare tell Bill. He would have been furious. He thinks it's all my imagination.' Lesley lapsed into silence.

A week later, the urgent appointment Dr Horley had made for Bobby to see the local paediatrician dropped through the letter-box. By this time Lesley was feeling a little more sure of herself, following the talk with her GP. She had explained to Bill that Dr Horley thought that Bobby's behaviour could be due to a specific disorder – and that her feelings of fear were quite understandable. Bill arranged for a morning off work so that he could attend the hospital with Lesley and Bobby. Bobby's behaviour that morning was especially bad. Bill admitted later that he had not realized the difficulties his wife had been facing.

'We'll just run a few blood-tests,' Dr Gibbs said, having heard the full story of Bobby's behaviour and previous history. 'But I am pretty certain that he is affected by ADD – and I'm not surprised you view him with a certain amount of caution, Mrs Peters! Bobby's getting a tough young man.'

One evening, six months later, Mrs Farley had just gone to bed. 'Gran's taking Bobby to the ice show tomorrow, Bill,' said Lesley. 'They're really good friends now, since we started on the treatment. What a good job you sent me to see Dr Horley. But I always knew there was nothing wrong with me!'

These events highlight how misunderstandings can arise over the true cause of a family's problems. If action had not been taken, the situation could have escalated into something far more serious, with Lesley's feelings becoming more intense and causing real problems in the relationship with her son and the rest of the family.

3 Disappointment

Parental disappointment with a child can be a destructive feeling – especially when the disappointment is due to such an obvious cause as bad behaviour. We all want our children to have successful lives. But the child with ADD seems set on a course of self-destruction, where the likelihood of success at anything seems to be becoming increasingly remote. The child's social life – and later his work possibilities – are, and will continue to be, affected by his impulsiveness, lack of concentration and hyperactivity.

Parents need help to understand their child's problems, so that they can develop realistic expectations of what he will be able to achieve. Forcing him to do something which is quite outside his capabilities will undoubtedly aggravate the symptoms associated with the condition. Self-esteem, already low in the child with ADD, will plummet even lower.

4   A nuisance?

Any child is all too aware if they sense that their parents regard them as a nuisance. The child who already has low self-esteem will be further upset by the 'messages' which are being sent – perhaps quite unconsciously. Again, reactions to this will be further bouts of bad behaviour. Once parents realize the extent to which their own actions and words can make the situation worse, they can take steps to alter this damaging attitude. It is essential that parents take time out from a demanding, badly behaved child – one evening a week, pursuing some hobby or other activity, can be a life-saver and can help to reduce negative feelings.

Knowing about the condition

Parents need to know as much as possible about the condition with which their child is affected, as an important prerequisite of starting any treatment. Written material on the causes, signs and symptoms, and treatment of ADD are of enormous help (whether notes made by the GP or health visitor, or books and articles) – as well as having an accessible, knowledgeable person with whom to talk through daily problems. Membership of a society, such as the ADD Family Support Group, can put parents in touch with others facing similar problems. Ways of coping with common difficulties can be shared, and often much can be learned from someone else's way of solving a specific problem.

Also, detailed knowledge of the reasons why certain behavioural techniques are used will help parents to carry them out successfully.

A lifelong condition

Part of knowing about ADD includes the understanding that it can never be cured. The sufferer can, however, be taught techniques to reduce the effects of the disorder – and eventually come to use these techniques herself. So in this context parents must fully understand the need for ongoing, long-term treatment.

Restoring the parents' self-esteem

The self-esteem of parents, as well as of children affected by ADD, can spiral downwards rapidly as bad behaviour continues. However much parents understand and are reassured, thoughts such as, 'Is it our fault?'; 'What have we done wrong?', can frequently rise, unbidden, to the surface. Paediatricians, health visitors, teachers, nursery staff and social workers all have a role to play in boosting parental morale.

The depth to which a parent's self-esteem has sunk depends on how long he or she has been struggling on alone, trying to cope with their difficult child. The very worst situation is when a parent is beginning to feel suicidal unless something changes soon. Urgent help is needed under these circumstances. A period of respite from the child's demands can often be a crucial necessity. On the positive side, however, it is surprising how quickly parents can return to normal once help has been given, and they can begin to see an improvement – however small – in their child's behaviour.

Sympathetic listening and support from many people – family and friends, as well as more professional counsellors – are just the first step in helping parents to see and understand the difficulties under which their child is living. It is only when they have fully grasped the basic principles of the necessary treatment that they can begin to supervise the modification of the child's behaviour at home. Parents must also recognize that progress may well be slow. Unusual events or situations may result in the child's returning to her previous unacceptable behaviour. It's vital that parents remain confident in the eventual good outcome, despite these temporary set-backs.

Behaviour modification

Behaviour modification is an enormous subject. Behaviour modification is a psychological tool which is used to change the existing patterns of a person's behaviour, and to help them learn new, more positive behaviour-patterns. It can be used in many situations – for example, to control outbursts of temper, or to help someone respond to everyday situations in a positive, rather than a negative, way. For ADD sufferers, behaviour modification is mainly used to improve concentration and to control hyperactivity.

Only broad guidelines can be suggested here, as each individual child differs in the way in which they are affected by ADD – and each home situation is similarly unique. One family may insist on regular meal-times and bedtimes for their children; the family next door may be more relaxed on this aspect of child-care, but may insist on everyone taking adequate physical exercise. The suggestions given here must therefore be applied in a way which is appropriate to the needs, patterns and 'rules' of each individual family. Each section must be thought through and related to each specific situation.

1 Parents in agreement

It is of the utmost importance that parents agree with each other on the way to handle their child's problem. If the child is getting different 'messages' from each parent, not only will there be no improvement, but the situation will deteriorate rapidly. As well as being confused, the alert child will quickly learn how to turn a variety of situations to his own advantage. Any child can be manipulative, and children with ADD can be especially adept at this.

Both parents must understand exactly what goals are being set. They must also agree on the path by which to reach each goal, and must follow this consistently. (Even if the parents disagree on some aspect of dealing with the child, this must be sorted out between the parents – out of his hearing.)

Remember, too, that other family members and close friends will need to have an idea of what is planned, together with the hoped-for outcome. Grandparents, who perhaps only see the child at iregular intervals, should be kept informed of events. Remember that they may have been extremely worried about their grandchild's behaviour and the effect this is having on the whole family. Explain to them the problems involved with ADD, and the basic lines of treatment which will eventually be suggested (described in this chapter, and in Chapters 7 and 8). Get their co-operation right from the start. Grandparents can often succeed in a difficult situation where parents, who are facing the problems daily, are swamped. Many children relate in a unique way to an older generation, and children affected by ADD are no exception.

The same approach must be used with other family members and close friends who have frequent contact with the child. They, too, need to have the situation explained, along with the behaviour modification techniques involved.

2 The importance of routine

A structured, predictable environment is essential if behaviour modification is to work for an ADD sufferer. Routine is all-important. Knowing exactly what is happening – and when – does much to focus the child's mind. Children whose main problem is an inability to concentrate will gradually learn the basic structure of the day, if this is firmly established and maintained. This process should be started in short, easy steps. As a simple example: encourage the child always to wash his hands before a meal; eventually this will become a part of the meal-time routine. Start slowly and gently, and don't get worried or upset if there are many failures before a particular routine becomes an accepted part of life.

Another example is to set an acceptable bedtime. This may seem an impossibility at first, as the child with ADD often has difficulty in sleeping anyway. Don't insist the child goes to sleep immediately. Encourage reading or other quiet pursuits in the child's bedroom at a specific time, and this will eventually become an accepted part of the bedtime routine.

With some children, **relaxation techniques** can be a valuable part of the bedtime routine – for example, getting the child to join in slow, deep-breathing exercises can help him to wind down after the day's activities. Make a game of this, and perhaps encourage all the family to take part.

Focusing techniques can also be useful in bedtime preparations. Take the opportunity when quietness reigns and encourage:

- listening to the sounds of daily life around – the kettle boiling, the dog barking, a clock striking, for example;
- smelling what is happening around – the supper cooking, new-mown grass or a sweet scented flower.
- touching – remembering the feel of a woolly jumper, the shape and weight of a pencil;
- looking at, and then holding in the mind, a favourite picture or the memory of an especially happy recent event.

By doing this the child's senses are being focused on everyday things in an attempt to improve concentration. Adult help is necessary to start the child using these techniques – but he should gradually learn to do these exercises for himself. They are valuable in later life too, to help in coping with stressful situations.

Helping the child to cope

Each individual with ADD has different times of the day when routine is the most difficult to accept – waking up in the morning or going to bed at night are often particularly difficult.

For children who are completely disorganized in the mornings, check out with them the most helpful and sensible sequence of events to follow at this difficult time of the day. If necessary write down a list, in order, of the routine tasks to be done – for example:

- get out of bed;
- wash, bath or shower;
- dress (write down the order in which clothes should be put on);
- brush hair;
- eat breakfast;
- clean teeth.

At first, the parent will have to go through the tasks with the child. Support should than gradually be withdrawn, letting the child take responsibility. A similar pattern can be worked out for the child who has greater problems at the end of the day. If one routine does not succeed, others should be tried until a suitable pattern is found.

Again there will probably be many set-backs – but when you stand back and review the general pattern of the child's behaviour over, say a month or two, you will also notice many success.

3 *Recognizing strengths and weaknesses*

Recognizing the child's strengths and weaknesses is an important and basic aspect of attempting to modify her behaviour. We are all better at some things than others – and children are no exception to this, including the youngster affected with ADD. Sometimes parents can have difficulties in knowing just what are their child's strengths – especially if the child excels at an activity which is outside their own interests and expectations. For example, a household which is interested in science or history may have difficulty in recognizing the expertise of their child with animals. If he had shown skill and interest in archaeology or period costume, for example, they would have recognized and valued this more readily. Focusing on the child's best abilities ensures that he will be able to succeed in some aspect of life. Similarly, try to avoid situations and activities which you know to be particularly difficult for him. For example, team games can be a nightmare for children with ADD. They find the concepts of sharing and taking turns difficult – and these are the essentials of all team games.

4 Physical exercise

Physical exercise is an important aspect of helping the hyperactive child – though the particular type of exercise must be carefully thought out. Rather than encouraging the child to take part in team activities at nursery or at school, more solitary sports should be encouraged if possible. Judo, martial arts, dancing, swimming – all under adult supervision, of course – are a few examples of suitable pastimes. Swimming is an especially good sport for ADD children. They have to learn, and practise, co-ordination between breathing and the movements of their arms and legs – and it is fun to do this!

Activities for two people, such as table-tennis, could also be used to help the child relate to another person, and join in an activity. Initially an adult should play with the child, but eventually other children can be encouraged to play, with adult supervision still available.

Emphasis on physical fitness can also be incorporated into a goal-setting exercise (with the added bonus of using up surplus energy). Running, swimming or cycling, as well as being excellent physical activities, can be used for setting clearly defined targets. For example, get the child to note down, over time, the improvement she has made in running or swimming a specific distance. This will:

- give her interest in persisting at the activity;
- promote her self-esteem;
- give her a sense of achievement;
- eventually give her recognition of her abilities from her peers.

It is important that an interested adult – parent, teacher, youth-leader, sports enthusiast – should show a good deal of interest in, and support of, these activities. While needing somewhat solitary sports, the child with ADD also needs plenty of encouragment to continue.

Regular times to pursue these sports must be fitted into the general routine of the day. If the child understands that, before very long, he will be able to use up his surplus energy doing something he enjoys, he is much more likely to concentrate on the task in hand.

5 Providing an escape route

An 'escape route' can be very reassuring to a child who is learning to control his own behaviour. It can take the form of either a place to be alone; or of someone outside the family to whom the children turn when feeling under extra stress.

Every child, if possible, should have a room of their own. Here he can be himself, without feeling under the continual scrutiny of an adult assessing his behaviour. It may be that he needs to sit quietly for a time, and not live up to everyone's expectations of continual hyperactivity. Or maybe he needs to take time over a special activity – drawing, music, modelling – depending on his own special interests. Beware, however, of providing a television or personal computer in his bedroom. He could watch television for long periods of time with very little good result. It is far better to encourage him to watch suitable programmes with the rest of the family – as part of the process of learning to mix well with other people. PCs, with a supply of computer games, can all too easily become an addiction. Used properly, these can have some educational merit – but only under supervision and for short periods of time.

Alongside their need to be alone sometimes, many children also need someone outside the immediate family to whom to turn. When life gets too busy or stressful at home, they can find temporary relief in a different environment. This is especially true for the ADD sufferer. This relationship with someone outside the immediate, day-to-day contacts at home can also help to relieve tensions in the family – tensions which inevitably arise as a result of the behaviour-patterns of the child affected by ADD. Being able to relax in the company of someone else will probably help a child to be more relaxed at home. Parents must, of course, know where, and to whom, their child is going – and the person offering this respite to child and family must also be aware of the nature of their difficulties.

Rachel's story

Rachel had been a strong-willed, but lovable, child right from the start. But when secondary school days loomed on the horizon, her behaviour became very stressful to the immediate family. Everything had to be done her way – and her room was a disaster-area. Her mother, Gill

Williams, was sometimes at her wit's end trying to instil some order into Rachel's life. 'How you will cope at your new school, Rachel, I just don't know!' she cried in exasperation one day. 'Don't want to go!' shouted Rachel, slamming the door in her mother's face.

'Where are you going, Rachel?' Gill called, seeing her daughter run off down the road towards the village.

A few minutes later the phone rang, and Gill heard the serene voice of her mother as she lifted the receiver. 'Rachel's here with me, Gill,' she said. 'I'll see she gets home safely when she's calmed down a bit.'

'Thank goodness mother came to live round the corner,' thought Gill. 'She has certainly been a boon to Rachel lately.' Over the preceding months Rachel had taken to arriving, breathless and often angry, at her grandmother's bungalow. Mrs Stevens would welcome her in, provide a drink, and maybe a chocolate biscuit (of which she seemed to have an inexhaustible supply), and just sit quietly with her. Maybe an afternoon TV programme would be on, and the two of them would watch this together. At other times they would share a quiet game of Patience, or Rachel would help her grandmother with some routine household task. But whatever they did, Rachel's bad mood always seemed to evaporate, and she would return home in a more reasonable frame of mind – until the next time the situation became fraught at home.

Regretfully a few months later Grandma Stevens died. The effect on Rachel was dramatic, and the family suffered many anxious years before Rachel finally settled down into a happy, successful adult. But that is another story . . .

While Rachel was not affected by ADD, she still needed to escape, temporarily, into a different environment. Children affected with ADD can also urgently need this form of safety valve.

6 One thing at a time

Parents must learn to concentrate on just one aspect of their child's unacceptable behaviour. There is no chance of each and every type of bad behaviour being 'cured' at once. For example, a good starting-point may be to concentrate on the need to be more organized when setting out in the morning. Check out the night before everything which will be needed for the next day at nursery or school. See that they are put together in an accessible place. In the morning, remind the child – gently but firmly – to check yet again that he has everything he will need throughout the day. (This can be made all part of the orderly start to the day.)

It may take many weeks before you notice any tangible success. But when the child arrives at nursery or school, on several consecutive days, with everything he needs, his self-esteem will be hugely boosted. Praise at this time is also vitally important. Later, you can use similar exercises to control his impulsive behaviour. Talking through the results of different actions can also be helpful. In this way the child learns that stopping to think really does pay off.

Rewards (however small) for success never come amiss. Perhaps a new school-bag, once everything has been collected together for a week or two? This is not bribery, but a way of showing your pleasure, and your commitment to giving your child help in overcoming the difficulties he faces as a result of ADD.

7 Encourage friendships

Friendships are important for all children. The child affected with ADD can have the greatest difficulty in making friends. Other children are wary of her impulsive and hyperactive behaviour. She is the last one to be chosen for a team game because of her impulsiveness and lack of concentration. She may also be shunned in the playground for these same reasons.

Parents can help with these situations in a number of ways:

- Inviting another child home after school for a specific purpose, such as an activity in which both children are interested. Close, but subtle, supervision is important in the early stages – any difficulties can then be side-tracked, and other activities suggested.
- It is usually sensible to invite the friend for a short time only at first. Remember the affected child's attention-span is short, and having to share with someone else is a strain at first. So from the outset, fix the time when the friend is to be collected, or taken home. Be immediately ready, too, to change to a different activity if you see that the initial one is getting boring or it is too difficult for your child to sustain concentration.
- Friendships blossom when similar interests are shared. It is worth taking time to investigate local facilities connected with your child's interests – and follow this up by taking her regularly to the appropriate meetings. This can take up much of a parent's leisure-time, and so will need to be carefully slotted in with other activities.

Parents must think carefully about the long-term implications: from the child's point of view, it is better never to have attended than to have to give up just when real interest has been sparked, and potentially long-lasting friendships made.

8 *Offer encouragement*

Finally, and perhaps most important of all, is the ongoing need to encourage the child on a regular basis. Praise for each and every small success must be given unreservedly. Failures, while not ignored nor condoned, should be played down, and encouragement offered that next time will be more successful. This may be no easy task for parents to sustain, when progress appears to be painstakingly slow. But remember that one positive word of praise is worth many words of reproach. It is better to retreat temporarily from a difficult situation than to engage in argument.

Coping with a child affected by ADD is never going to be easy. Just remembering all the ways in which you can offer him help to modify his behaviour can seem a vast undertaking in itself. But as the weeks and months pass, you will establish new habits of handling potentially difficult situations. As his behaviour improves, so also will daily life at home. You will once again begin to enjoy your child's company.

Summary

- Parents need counselling to gain knowledge and understanding of ADD;
- behaviour modification can in many simple ways, help to improve a child's behaviour;
- progress can be slow;
- long-term strategies will be needed.

7

How to cope at school

For parents, days at school come as a welcome relief from the need to cope with their child affected by attention deficit disorder (ADD) on an hourly basis. These feelings are eminently understandable! But never forget that treatment must involve all the professionals in a child's life – and parents are the most central and vital 'professionals' of all. Liaison between home and school must be very close to establish a unified method of handling the child's difficulties.

Before discussing ways of handling children at school, let us look at the particular difficulties which an ADD sufferer may face at school.

ADD and problems at school

1   *Impact on learning*

For a child to be able to take full advantage of any school, a number of conditions must be met:

- teaching must be good, and of a level suitable to the child's understanding;
- a child must be at the right developmental level (not necessarily the same thing as the chronological age) to benefit from teaching;
- the child must also have the ability to concentrate fully on the learning material provided.

This final condition cannot be met by the child affected by ADD. Hyperactivity and impulsive behaviour also cause major disruption to the learning process. For example, a child needs a fair degree of concentration to learn about such everyday concepts as weight, shape and colour. Children with ADD will first of all have problems in being aware of exactly what is expected of them – in addition, their excessive activity makes it impossible for them to learn properly. And if this type of situation continues for any length of time, the child will start to fall behind his peers in basic learning. The inevitable result is a poor performance which fails to reflect his actual intelligence and abilities. This can become evident even at an early age, in a playgroup, nursery or reception class. Unless the problems are recognized and steps taken to remedy them, this under-achievement can continue, and become progressively worse, as school days advance.

From the teacher's point of view, it is just not possible to devote extra time and attention to one child when the whole class has to be controlled and taught. The problems of the one disruptive child need to be recognized, and he must be given appropriate help, with added input from many other people. One untreated hyperactive child in a class can cause ripples of chaos throughout the day.

2   Disorganization

The general disorganization of the child's life can also have an impact on the school day. Certain basic requirements are needed before children fit neatly into the pattern of a school – for example, children must be able to dress themselves without too much help from an adult. The child with ADD is quite capable of performing these day-to-day activities, but just cannot concentrate for long enough to be able to do them adequately. So he will come out of school with shoes undone, coat unbuttoned and the latest – unfinished – offering from the day's activities trailing in the road.

A child with ADD regularly forgets to tell her parents about any needs for the following day. Notes are lost, equipment or clothes mislaid, and important events forgotten. All children show these tendencies at some time, of course – especially during the early school years, when everything is strange and new. But the child affected by ADD rarely has any success in controlling and organizing their lives.

Play materials can also cause problems. Paints, glue, and other aids to learning, are messy – children need adequate protection for clothes while they are working with these materials, and most manage quite successfully to emerge clean and tidy. Not so the hyperactive child: paint and glue will somehow transfer themselves to every part of his anatomy and clothing, as well as being spattered all over the surrounding area – and, at worst, over other children. This is not deliberate on his part – it is merely that he is so energetic and impulsive that he cannot possibly take the necessary care.

3   Easily distracted

Being all day in the company of other children can also bring to light the distractibility of the ADD child. He is always the child who turns round when another child sneezes, and he is the one who always has to look at, and find out about, the activities of others. His own work suffers as a result – not that he would have stuck at it anyway, for no sooner had he started it than something else more exciting would claim his attention. All these things have an ongoing effect on learning ability.

4   Friendship problems

The symptoms of ADD can also mean that the sufferer finds it hard to make friends. After a short time, other children will tire of her hyperactive behaviour and impulsiveness – she will often have spoilt their work by her intrusions, and this in itself does not lead to feelings of companionship. Her constant interruptions during stories and in other quiet activities will also become irritating, after a while. The effects of all this are that initially the affected child behaves worse and worse, in a vain attempt to gain popularity. She may then become lonely and withdrawn, and anxiety and depression can then ensue to worsen the child's unhappy feelings. Self-esteem can reach an all-time low if the problems are not recognized and given appropriate treatment.

The four problem-areas described above, together with many other examples of the behaviour of the child with ADD, can have serious and far-reaching effects on his school career. In fact, it is often not until his early school or nursery days that a positive diagnosis is made. It is at this stage of life that the affected child is seen to be very different from his peers in terms of his day-to-day behaviour.

The Code of Practice

So what can be done in schools to cope with the child affected by ADD? Before discussing the detailed techniques, we shall look briefly at the Code of Practice which resulted from the 1993 Education Act in Britain. This Code gives practical advice and guidance to schools – and governors of schools – about their responsibilities for children with 'special educational needs'. This phrase covers a vast array of problems ranging from mobility problems, deafness, visual problems and learning difficulties, to mention just a few. ADD is just one among many reasons for realizing that a child has 'special educational needs'.

It is estimated that up to 20 per cent of school-age children will have 'special needs' at some time or other during their school careers. These needs may only be temporary – for example, a broken leg, which requires special attention for only a short time. For others, however, the disability is long-lasting and requires special help – perhaps throughout a whole school career and subsequent working life (for example, sufferers from cerebral palsy, blindness or profound deafness from birth). Children with ADD are classed as having 'special educational needs' – but with appropriate help, especially if it is given in the early years before extra bad habits are formed as a result of the original problem, they may well be able to follow a normal school career. Review at frequent intervals throughout their school career will be necessary.

The basic principles of the Code of Practice state that:

1   All special needs must be recognized and addressed throughout the child's school career;
2   National Curriculum requirements must be satisfied for all children whatever the special need;
3   Most children with special needs should be accommodated in mainstream schools;
4   Partnership with parents must be a priority;
5   Pre-school children can also be recognized as having special needs.

These features again emphasize the need for the co-ordinated involvement of a number of different professionals with all children with special needs. The recognition of a 'special need' before statutory school age will, for example, involve staff from the health service and also possibly social services. In this way, schools can be alerted early on to the special facilities which will be needed when a child reaches school age.

Every school in Britain has on the staff a teacher known as a special educational needs co-ordinator. This teacher ideally has a wide knowledge of many types of special need, and of the facilities locally to cater for those needs. This is a mammoth task, bearing in mind all the different 'needs', both temporary and permanent, which can occur. Help can only be given within the framework of the facilities available locally, and within the educational budget – another problem-area. The tasks of the special educational needs co-ordinator include:

1   Close liaison between school and home so that (in the case of children with ADD) both parents and teachers pursue basically the same pattern of behaviour-control. This can be especially helpful to

both parents and teachers, as messages passed on through the child can be, to say the least, unreliable.

2 The co-ordination of, and adherence to, as far as is possible locally, the principles set out in the Code of Practice.

3 The development of in-service training for teachers in the care and management of children with a wide range of special needs. Days set aside for the discussion of specific difficulties, and led by outside speakers, are just one way of ensuring that teachers know as much as possible regarding a particular condition. Other, more local, ways of offering help are also discussed.

4 Making and updating a register of all the children with special needs in the school.

5 Liaison with other agencies – health services, social services, therapists of all kinds – who are also involved in the welfare of the child.

These tasks sound formidable, but can be made manageable if everyone involved with each specific child helps each other, and shares knowledge and experience. Parents must be made aware of the special needs advisory service in their child's school. The policy regarding special educational needs, as it applies to their child, should also be explained to them. It is important that all parents of a child with special needs fully understand these policies – for example, if a parent's first language is not English, an interpreter should be used if necessary.

As a result of discussions with all the carers and professionals regarding an individual child's difficulties, an 'individual education plan' is drawn up by the special needs co-ordinator. This includes:

1 A special plan – daily, weekly and termly – for each child who is considered to have special educational needs.

2 An in-depth assessment of individual strengths and weaknesses carried out by all involved with the child at school, together with any relevant comments from parents regarding behaviour at home.

3 Extra advice and help from specialists, such as speech therapists, or psychologists, or experts in other areas in which the child is considered to need extra help.

4 Involvement of parents – and the child – in the decision-making process. This will improve the links between home and school activities.

It is important that a specific date is set for a review of progress. This review should include all the reports and thoughts of everyone involved with the child on a day-to-day basis.

If an individual education plan simply seems inadequate (despite the best efforts of all concerned), a further procedure – known as 'statementing' – is put into motion. This means that, with the help of a multi-disciplinary team, the local education authority (LEA) makes a statutory assessment of the individual child's special needs. When all reports and suggestions have been received, the LEA officers decide on the best future education for the child. The parents are an important part of this assessment procedure, and can disagree at any stage with the LEA's proposals as to their child's future education.

Possible different methods of education include:

1 A change of school to one where the particular needs of the child can be more successfully met.

2 Further outside help in response to the advice given on an individual education plan – for example, extra speech therapy. This can be especially necessary for children with ADD as they may need specific help to express their ideas verbally.

3 Exclusion from school may be necessary, if bad behaviour has been too severe to handle in the normal school situation and the education of other children is thought to be suffering. In this case, admission to a different school may be suggested, or, as an emergency measure, home tuition on a one-to-one basis may be advised.

4 As a last resort, attendance at either a day or residential school for children with behavioural difficulties can be advised. This need not last for the remainder of the child's school career. A short time in an appropriate special school may be all that is needed to set behaviour-patterns which can again be managed in a mainstream school setting.

The above is a brief description of the legislation in Britain for children with special educational needs. Details vary from area to area – and other countries have different methods of assessment and subsequent education. Basic principles are, however, similar – as are the individual ways of handling of behavioural difficulties in the classroom.

To summarize:

- Initially, special difficulties can be sorted out by the class teacher;
- next the special educational needs co-ordinator gets involved;
- finally, there is an assessment by a multi-disciplinary team, with possible statementing procedures.

Parents must be involved at each and every stage, and their permission obtained before any specialist sees their child.

General guidelines for managing ADD at school

There is no one educational programme that will fit all the needs of every child with ADD. Each child must be assessed individually, and the specific problems recognized and addressed when making the educational plan. The suggestions given below are general, and must be adapted to fit in with the individual requirements of each child.

Physical safety must be one of the prime considerations for all teachers concerned with ADD children. This must include the safety of all the other pupils, and the staff, as well as the individual child. Impulsive behaviour can involve other people in dangerous situations. The mere impulsiveness of running across a classroom at an inappropriate time can cause damage to other children, or to equipment which happens to be in the way. During later school days, when delicate and perhaps expensive equipment is being used, damage can become a major problem.

PE classes must also be carefully controlled. Basic equipment can be a temptation for a hyperactive child – and much damage can be done to the child, and to those around, if such equipment is not used properly and under supervision.

In the younger age-group, pieces of equipment such as scissors can be a danger in the wrong – i.e. hyperactive – hands. Teachers must constantly monitor their use, and remember not to leave them lying around on a table. Good classroom organization is an important factor in keeping safety standards high. Teachers should, if possible, try to anticipate the impulsive actions of the ADD child. Many accidents, both indoors and outside, start from an impulsive act.

Classroom assistants, if available, are invaluable in helping to ensure physical safety, as well as helping with other aspects of behaviour modification – though it can be difficult to obtain such help when financial resources are limited. However, it is not only the hyperactive child who benefits from the extra help available; the whole class benefits from a more controlled atmosphere – and teachers will find stress-levels lowered.

As at home, the need for a structured school day is of vital importance. This can involve both the way in which the physical space in the classroom is organized, and the appropriate timetabling of the day's work.

1 The physical organization of the classroom

The aim is to reduce distractions for the ADD child as far as possible. By doing this, he will more easily be able to concentrate on the task in hand. For example, if a child sits near a low window overlooking a busy road, or a field containing a herd of cows, there is an overwhelming temptation to disregard what is going on in the classroom. Most children would find this difficult – but for the child with ADD, attention to anything inside the room would be almost an impossibility. A noisy heater, or squeaky door, can also provide plenty of opportunity for distraction. The possibilities are endless.

Adequate room on a table – or between desks – is also a must for an ADD pupil. When other children's books, papers, pencils, paints, intrude upon his space – or when his equipment intrudes on another area – once again the scene for disruption is set. Teachers must ensure, though, that any extra space given to the affected child is not obvious to other children. This can be seen as favouritism, and so further isolate the child from his peers.

It is a sensible idea to have the ADD child sitting near the front of the room or near the teacher's desk, depending on the lay-out of the room. The child will then have to make a deliberate effort to look at other distractions in the room. In addition, the teacher is more easily able to monitor her activity, and also to help her concentrate on the task in hand. Placing the quietest, most placid children in the class nearby will also reduce unwelcome distractions. The aura of quietness, and lack of unnecessary movement, can have a calming effect on the child.

Remember that ADD children have most difficulty in changing, and relatively unstructured, situations. Time should be given for them to settle into a different routine after, for example, lunch-break or play-time.

For older children, a separate study-booth or carrel is the ideal situation in which to work. Under these circumstances, however, care must be taken that the child is actually pursuing the prescribed course of study, and not following his own interests.

Teachers should ensure that the child knows exactly where to sit, where to put books, pencils and other needed articles, as well as where he will be expected to go at the end of the session. Children with ADD are often anxious – and uncertainty about present, and future, events can add to their burden.

2   Managing time

With the very short attention-span of many children with ADD, it is important that they learn to manage time. This needs to be taught in short steps, with adequate reinforcement at each stage.

Short bursts of instruction, interwoven with other activities, is the ideal for an ADD child. The timetable for such a student will probably need subtle alteration from that used by the rest of the class. The ideal is to alternate quiet and active sessions.

Teachers adept at dealing with hyperactive children will have a number of alternative tasks readily available. For example, when the teacher sees that the child is having difficulty in concentrating on the current task, she may sent him to tidy the bookshelf, run an errand or to pass round papers – thus avoiding a disruptive outburst.

It is specially important for the teacher to plan the day's activities in advance. The basic original plan should be stuck to, adding in extra activities if the situations seem to be getting explosive.

The teacher should set aside time to go over any instructions several times, either orally or in writing – which will cement the instructions in the child's mind. With lack of persistent concentration, the child may miss one small, but important, piece of information, which can make nonsense of the whole of the request.

Teachers must remember that children with ADD need time to respond to questions (and also to start on various tasks) – time to sort out a sensible response, rather than coming out with an impulsive and confused reply.

Specific help from teachers

Teaching skills are necessary for educating all children – but to teach ADD children, these skills must be honed to allow for the particular problems of the pupil. The following are a few examples of strategies for dealing with potentially difficult situations:

- Teachers should give visual, or physical, cues to the child when a certain response is required. These cues need to be agreed with the child previously, and could include, for example, direct eye-contact,

63

a raised eyebrow, or a gentle hand on the shoulder when a specific response is necessary. The child's attention is thereby brought back to the task in hand. Such cues also give the child extra confidence.

- It is important to know when to back off from a situation when teaching an ADD child. A teacher insisting that the child complete a task can be counterproductive if he is in an explosive state, or is obviously having problems in controlling impulsive or hyperactive behaviour. Instead, the teacher should suggest a different activity for a short while, getting the child to return to the original task later.

- Teachers should also recognize the child's need for 'time out'. For example, a request for a message to be taken to another classroom is a useful way of removing the child from an especially difficult situation.

- Teachers can provide the child with a list of articles needed for future activities, where these activities are to take place and when; this can help a child who has difficulty in organizing his time and space.

- There is a need to keep spare articles and equipment for use by the child who has – yet again – forgotten his own.

- Perhaps a good conduct report could be produced by school at regular intervals? Here, various aspects of the daily activities could be listed, ticked and commented on if they have been done successfully. Emphasis on success is of particular importance to the child with a low self-esteem due to previous continual failure.

- It is vital that teachers keep in close touch with the parents. The techniques practised both at school and at home must be consistent. Both teachers and parents will gain much support from regular meetings to discuss successes and failures, as well as to plan future ways of helping the child to cope with the problems.

Daniel's story

'It's not working, is it, Linda?' Ann Brown sat down wearily on the chair nearest the window in the staff-room. From this vantage point she could see easily into the playground. Children from Years 1 and 2 ran hither and thither, happily laughing and talking – apart from one small group. Here, the playground supervisor had once more had to step in and sort out a quarrel between six-year-old Daniel Brown and another small boy.

'Look at him now,' Ann sighed, 'in trouble again!' Linda Wagstaff, deputy head of St Leonard's First School, regarded her visitor sympathetically.

Daniel had recently been diagnosed as having ADD. A team-approach, involving behaviour modification techniques, and used both at home and at school, had been advised by the local psychologist. Teachers, parents, dinner-ladies and many others had all been primed as to how best to help Daniel and his mother.

For a short while there had seemed to be a slight improvement in Daniel's impulsive and hyperactive behaviour – but, as Ann Brown had just remarked, no further advances were being made. In fact, things were as bad as they ever were before the diagnosis of ADD had been made.

'Perhaps I should have agreed to the medicine that Dr Franks wanted to give Dan. But it seems wrong to me to give medicine to children just because they behave badly. What do you think, Linda? I've no one to talk to about it since Dan's father left us.' 'Why don't you go and discuss it again with Dr Franks?' suggested Linda. 'I'm sure he will understand why you have been so reluctant to give Dan the medication. But I do know that it had a remarkably good effect on a boy at my previous school,' she added.

Ann Brown managed to get a morning appointment to see Dr Franks, the paediatrician at the local hospital, within two weeks. It had been decided over the phone that she should go along without Daniel on this occasion. 'We shall be able to talk more quietly, Mrs Brown,' Dr Franks had said. 'You can tell me all the problems you are having with Daniel.'

'What about this drug Ritalin, Dr Franks?' asked Ann when the initial discussion about Daniel had finished. 'It doesn't seem right to me to give medicine to a healthy little boy.'

'It's true that Daniel is very healthy, but he does have a problem.' Dr Franks sat back and regarded Ann sympathetically. 'As you well know! Remember, he doesn't want to be always dashing around from one activity to another, upsetting everyone and having no friends. But his brain is continually being bombarded by all the things that are going on around him. He can't shut them out like we can. And this makes it impossible for him to concentrate on any one thing. Just imagine if you were unable to shut out all the noises going on outside now – in the corridor, in the road, the child crying next door. It would be mayhem.' Ann nodded. 'Would Ritalin cure this?' she asked.

'Ritalin – which is a very safe drug – does not cure ADD, but it will enable Daniel to concentrate better and to ignore most of the outside activity. We would start with the lowest dosage, and then only increase it gradually until we found the best dosage for him.'

Ann sat up straight, her decision made. 'Yes,' she said firmly. 'Let's try it, please. I can't go on much longer coping with Dan's behaviour.'

'Right.' Dr Franks drew his prescription pad towards him. 'Get these from the pharmacy. Carry on with the behaviour modifications we all agreed on. And come and see me next week – with Dan.'

The following Tuesday morning dawned sunny and bright. Ann Brown and Daniel walked into Dr Frank's consulting room with a spring in both their steps and a smile on both their faces.

'School's fun, Dr Franks,' announced Daniel, taking a seat beside his mother. 'And my friend Toby is coming to tea today!' Dr Franks raised an enquiring eyebrow in Ann Brown's direction. 'Marvellous!' she said, softly.

Ritalin doesn't always have such a marked, immediate effect as it obviously had on Daniel. Dosage often has to be adjusted until the right amount is found. But occasionally such spectacular results are seen even with the minimum dose.

Homework

Homework can be a fraught subject for the child with ADD. If he actually remembers to take it home, there can be enormous problems over what should be done, and when it should be ready – never mind actual settling down to do it. Initially the teacher should expect only small amounts of work. It should also be agreed that parental help and involvement is permissible – not that the parents should present a piece of work completely entirely by themselves, but rather that they should help the child to settle down to think about and then to put down on paper the tasks set.

It can be suggested to parents that several short spells of homework are probably preferable to one long session. Also, homework should never be left until late in the evening. As well as being tired after the day's activities, the child may have greater difficulties than usual in getting to sleep if homework is done just before bedtime.

Summary

Dealing with a hyperactive child, who has concentration problems and is also impulsive, can create major difficulties at school. Not only must the best be done for the individual child, but all the other children in the class must not miss out on teaching because of one pupil's disruptive behaviour.

Scheduling and routine, with thought for alternative activities to counteract difficult situations, underpin good practice under these circumstances. This, together with the co-operation of other professionals and parents, will eventually produce results. It must always be remembered that there is no cure for ADD – only techniques which children and their carers can learn to help them manage their particular problems. Much responsibility for this lies with good, specialized, consistent teaching practice.

In short:

- ADD has an impact on learning ability;
- friendships can run into difficulty;
- in Britain, special educational needs teachers play a vital role;
- physical safety, both of children and staff, is a prime consideration;
- classroom organization is important;
- it is essential that the ADD sufferer learns to manage time;
- extra teaching skills are necessary;
- good liaison with home, and other professionals, is vital.

8

Medication

There is no medication which will magically alter the behaviour of a child affected by attention deficit disorder (ADD). Drugs are just one part of the range of treatment available, the most significant part of which is behaviour modification techniques (described in Chapter 6), which are used in each and every situation in the child's life. There are, however, several drugs which can be used alongside behaviour modification, and which, in some children, have excellent results.

General points about drug treatments

Before discussing the different drugs used in the treatment of ADD, we must consider a few general points about ongoing drug treatment for children. Firstly, it is important that doctors find out what the parents' views are about on long-term drug therapy – perhaps especially when mind-altering (psychotropic) drugs are being used. Doctors must address the parents' secret fears about drugs which seem to alter the child's basic personality – even if for the better! Parents may question whether or not they should allow their son or daughter to be prescribed these drugs at all. They may also worry about whether the medicine is addictive, especially if it has to be used over a considerable period of time.

These are sensible questions which need honest answers. No one would choose to have their child taking medicine on a daily basis – whether it be for an illness such as diabetes, or to control the convulsions of epilepsy. But in both these cases, the drugs are needed to relieve an abnormal condition – in some cases, a life-threatening one. The same argument can be used for the need for drugs of the child with ADD. The sufferer does not want to be in constant trouble – and possibly friendless – because of his impulsiveness and lack of concentration skills. So if there is a drug available which can help to control these characteristics, it is surely sensible that it should be used to enable the child to grow up happily, and develop his full potential.

Side-effects can occur, as with any drug. But as long as these are reported by parents, and closely monitored by the prescribing doctor, they can be minimized either by altering the dosage or changing to a different drug. The effects and effectiveness of the drug (as well as its side-effects) must be closely checked. Is it really giving the hoped-for effect? Or are the benefits only marginal? Liaison with nursery or school staff is important here: the child's behaviour may differ markedly at school from at home. Many different people are in contact with the child during the course of a week, and all their observations are of value. Unless progress is monitored, it will be difficult to find the most suitable drug for each individual child.

Liaison is also important, over a longer time-span, when it comes to dosage. As a child grows, the dose of any medication will probably need to be adjusted. So teachers must inform parents if the child is regressing to more difficult behaviour. This may highlight the need for a change of dosage – or maybe a change of drug.

As to the parents' worry about their child's possible addiction to the drugs being used to control the symptoms of his ADD – they can be reassured. There is no evidence that the drugs used for this condition are addictive.

Drugs and the child

The affected child, too, needs explanations as to why she has to take pills when none – or hardly any – of her peers do so. All children like to conform, and to be taking medicine is not the norm for most children. A knowledgeable friend or close relative is probably the best person to explain this. The child can easily pick up on a parent's negative feelings if an involved, worried father or mother does the explaining. A calm, down-to-earth explanation is the ideal, without undue emphasis on the importance of the medication. It should be treated as a fact of life – like eating or brushing teeth. The child's subsequent questions must also be answered with complete honesty. And remember that explanations have to be consistent, so parents should check on the exact information which the child has been given.

Some of the drugs used must be given at frequent intervals – four-hourly with the most commonly used ones. This can give rise to problems when the child is at school all day long, and a dose of medicine is required at lunch-time. Schools vary in their approach to teachers being responsible for giving medicine during the school day. If there is no school nurse available, parents may be required to oversee the lunch-time dose themselves – either by bringing the child home for lunch, or by visiting the school at the appropriate time. This is yet another, very necessary part of the liaison process between everyone involved with the child on a daily basis.

A further point to be considered by both parents and doctors on the subject of whether there are any adolescent children in the family. Some of the drugs used to control ADD are powerful stimulants, which can be very attractive to teenagers wanting to experiment. Parents must be warned of this possibility if a younger child is having such drugs prescribed.

The drugs available

There are currently two main groups of drugs being used in the treatment of ADD. The stimulant group of drugs is the most commonly used, and offers an effective means of controlling symptoms. They help focus the child's attention, so controlling the impulsiveness that is such a feature of ADD.

Other types of drug, with varying actions, can also be used, either as an alternative for individual children or as an added medication if this is thought to be necessary.

Research is continuing for an ideal drug to control the symptoms of ADD. This would:

• have day-long activity;
• have no, or few, side-effects;
• suit the majority of sufferers;
• lack the potential for abuse;
• be inexpensive.

No drug at present fulfils all these ideals – and perhaps one will never be found. Meanwhile, a range of the available drugs may be tried to find out which best suits each individual child.

Stimulant drugs

Ritalin

Ritalin (whose generic name is methylphenidate) is the most commonly used drug for the treatment of ADD. It is available in two forms: a short-acting one, lasting four hours, and a longer-acting one, lasting up to eight hours. It is not available in liquid form, so children have to be able to swallow tablets. The short-acting type can be crushed and given in a favourite food. The longer-acting – which has obvious advantages for the timing of the doses – cannot be crushed and so must be swallowed. This drug should not be used for children under the age of six.

The initial dose of Ritalin is 5 mg a day, and this can be raised up to a maximum of 20 mg a day. It is vitally important that parents and teachers keep a close watch until the correct dose for each individual is established. This is often a fine balance between a dose which modifies behaviour adequately but without causing side-effects.

The first dose of the day must be given early in the morning, and effects will be seen in as short a time as 20 minutes. With the short-acting type, a further dose is necessary at lunch-time. The drug is stopped at night and started afresh each morning.

Side-effects can occur, and again must be carefully watched for. These include:

- mild sleep disturbance;
- loss of appetite;
- mild irritability;
- occasional twitching (tics).

If you, as a parent, are concerned about the way in which any of these side-effects are affecting your child, talk to your GP about changing the dosage, or moving the child on to another drug. Minor side-effects can be avoided by taking the following steps:

- The sleep disturbance can be reduced by ensuring that the child's last dose of the day is taken well before bedtime. Many children seem to be able to manage very adequately with a morning dose, followed by a smaller dose at lunch-time – this is sufficient to last the whole day. The side-effect of sleep disturbance is thus rarely a problem.
- Loss of appetite can be avoided by giving the Ritalin either immediately before, or even with, a meal. However, if the child loses his appetite to the extent that he is not gaining weight steadily along normal lines – or is actually losing weight – mention this to your GP so that an alternative to Ritalin can be tried.
- Irritability can often be controlled by avoiding the 'triggering' situations known to parents or teachers. This can be dealt with

alongside the other behaviour modification techniques being followed. If emotional upsets occur too often, discuss with your GP the possibilities of reducing the dosage or changing to another drug.

• Tics – such as facial grimaces, shrugging of the shoulders and blinking – can usually be controlled by lowering the dose of Ritalin. If, however, Tourette syndrome (in which these and other tics are a major difficulty) is an added problem in an individual child, and Ritalin is making the tics worse, a different drug should be tried.

Ritalin has an excellent safety-record. It can cause dramatic improvement in behaviour in a very short time for many children with ADD. Trials have shown that around 80 per cent of children affected by the disorder benefit from Ritalin.

However, Ritalin – along with any other drug used – should only be used alongside, and to support, behaviour modification techniques. No drug for ADD should be given in isolation from other types of treatment. Also, the diagnosis of ADD must be confirmed accurately before any medication is prescribed. No drug should be given in a hit-and-miss attempt to cure unacceptable behaviour.

Dexedrine

Dexedrine (generic name, dextro-amphetamine) is another stimulant drug which, surprisingly, has the paradoxical effect of calming hyperactive behaviour. This drug is available in a liquid form as well as tablet form. It can also be given to children from the age of three. Again, it has a short action – around four hours – and so has to be given at intervals throughout the day. Again, dosage varies for each individual child, the initial dose being 5 mg, which is increased if necessary, over a period of time, if the desired effects are not being maintained.

Possible side-effects are similar to those seen with Ritalin – mild sleep disturbance, loss of appetite and irritability. Dexedrine also has a good safety-record.

Pemoline

Pemoline (trade-names Cylert and Volital) is a longer-acting drug – up to about eight hours. It is not recommended for children under the age of six. It is available in tablet form and, as with other drugs, it improves concentration and reduces mood swings.

Side-effects can include abdominal pain, with an associated loss of appetite which can lead to loss of weight, or failure to gain weight.

Pemoline is not such a safe drug as Ritalin or Dexedrine. Liver-damage is a remote possibility, and in view of this, blood-tests are done every six months – or, of course, before this time if there are symptoms – to check on liver function.

These three drugs are all stimulant drugs. Their action allows the affected child to focus more readily on the tasks in hand. Parents find that, on these drugs, their child:

- is more able to co-operate in normal family life;
- able to stick to – and even finish – the activity he has started;
- is less impulsive, and so will consider the results of any action – within the limits of his developmental level.

In short, life at home is calmer for the whole family, thanks to the effects of these drugs (used alongside other treatments) on the ADD sufferer.

At school, teachers note that, on these drugs, the child is:

- more able to finish successfully a piece of set work, in a neater and more presentable form than previously;
- less fidgety than previously. Other children's activities are less likely to be a distraction;
- better at making friends – and therefore at enjoying the free time in the playground.

Other drugs

There are two other drugs which can be used in the treatment of ADD – Tofranil (trade-name Imipramine) and Clonidine (trade-name Catapres).

Tofranil

Tofranil has been used for other childhood and adult problems – bed-wetting in children and depression in adults. Again, the dosage must be tailored to fit each individual child, the maximum effect being achieved with the lowest possible dose. Tofranil is longer-acting than most of the stimulant drugs. Often only one dose per day is required – a major advantage when the child is at school all day long. It may take up to two to three weeks before the full effect of the drug is seen. During this time a strict check must be kept on its effect on the child's behaviour. Blood-levels of the drug may also need to be checked from time to time (through blood-tests). Tofranil is particularly valuable if the child is also showing signs of depression, in addition to, or because of, ADD.

Side-effects include tiredness and headaches – and occasionally constipation can be a problem. Serious side-effects of irregular heart-beats can occur with much too high a dose of Tofranil, but this is exceedingly rare. In this instance, the child may complain of a 'bumpy' heart, and you will feel that the pulse is irregular.

This drug can be useful for children who are seriously affected by the side-effects of Ritalin.

Clonidine

Clonidine is a drug used to lower blood-pressure in adults. It is especially useful in controlling hyperactivity without causing tics to develop – or to worsen, if the child is also affected by Tourette syndrome.

This drug comes in tablet-form, and again dosage is very individual. Like Ritalin, it is short-acting – up to around four to six hours – so an extra dose may be needed at lunch-time. It is helpful to use this drug in children under the age of 12 in addition to other drugs.

Side-effects include excessive fatigue, a dry mouth and possible dizziness due to its action in lowering the blood-pressure.

Drugs – further considerations

The above are the common drugs in current use in the treatment of ADD. Research is going ahead, especially in the USA, to find an ideal drug. But again it must be emphasized that medication is only a part of the treatment of this disorder. Behaviour modification is the corner-stone of treatment: medication simply allows these techniques to be used more readily and effectively.

The question will undoubtedly arise as to how long treatment with drugs will be necessary. No single answer can be given for each individual child. For some children, a year will be sufficient for behavioural techniques to work with the help of drugs – while others may require the medication until they leave school. Parents are in the best position to monitor the effects of the drug. In most families, a dose of medicine will be forgotten occasionally for at least one day. Parents will then be able to see if there is any marked deterioration in their child's behaviour. If they do not notice any difference, they can try stopping the drug for a week – under medical supervision.

Remember, too, that it is the parent's decision alone that their child should be taking drugs for ADD.

Finally, a word about the dangers of any drugs.

- These should always be kept in a locked cupboard, well out of reach of any young children.
- A drug prescribed for one member of the family must never be used for another member.
- Any left-over drug – perhaps if the medication has been changed, for example – must be thrown away, or returned to the GP's surgery, to the hospital or the pharmacy.

Summary

- No single drug is available to cure children with ADD;
- parents must agree with any drug treatment;
- parents must be made aware of any possible side-effects;
- specific drugs, with their actions and side-effects, must be closely monitored not only by parents, but also by teachers and other carers.

9

Adults with attention deficit disorder

It has only relatively recently been recognized that attention deficit disorder (ADD) can persist into adult life. Some experts have estimated that around 30 per cent of children diagnosed as having ADD will continue to have problems in later life. Few studies of ADD in adults have, as yet, been carried out, so it is impossible to say precisely just how many adults are affected. One study, for example, suggested that the number of adult sufferers was much less than 30 per cent of childhood sufferers. The researchers came to the conclusion that the rate of ADD appears to decline by around 50 per cent every five years. So, if about 3 per cent of children are affected, only about 0.05 per cent of 40 year-olds will be sufferers. But another study suggested that around 3 per cent of the total adult population could be affected – about the same proportion of adults as children, in other words. Both of these studies were undertaken in America.

What has, however, been frequently noted is that although far more boys than girls suffer from ADD, this gender difference does not continue into adult life. It seems that the sexes are equally affected by ADD in adult life.

If it is accepted tht ADD is caused by a hereditary fault affecting the chemical transmission of messages in the brain, it is perhaps not surprising that ADD is found in adults. There are a number of possible reasons for the seemingly lower occurrence-rate of ADD in older age-groups:

- personality variations tend to determine whether or not ADD becomes a problem in later life;
- if the condition is successfully managed in childhood, this can help the affected person cope with their impulsivity and lack of concentration later.
- the lack of recognition of the condition in adults. The sufferer may just be labelled as lazy, immature, and lacking in enterprise and motivation, for example.

But whatever the exact rate of occurrence, it is highly probable that a significant number of adults is affected by this disorder.

Signs and symptoms

Signs and symptoms of ADD in adults are somewhat different from those seen in children. The basic difficulties of impulsiveness, and poor concentration and maybe also hyperactivity, are present – but coping techniques (often learned through difficult trial-and-error methods throughout childhood and adolescence) will have blurred the outlines of the ADD symptoms seen in children. Life experiences – good and bad – will certainly have altered the behaviour-patterns which are so clearly seen in children.

Adults with ADD can show one or more of the following difficulties:

- They are easily distracted – this seems to be as major a problem in adult life as in childhood. Working in an open-plan office is almost an impossibility for them. Any nearby movement or unusual activity will quickly, and repeatedly, claim their attention, distracting them from their work.

- They are generally disorganized. This is incompatible with a job which requires follow-through and attention to detail. Also, trains and buses are missed, and general necessary equipment can be mislaid. Their lack of organization in the home can also cause difficulties. Meals are haphazard, and rarely appear on time – and again, vital pieces of equipment are lost, or never bought at all due to forgetfulness – which is often a prominent feature. In a general sense, the whole family can be seen to suffer.

- As a result of the above attributes, the ADD sufferer often has employment problems. She probably has frequent job-changes, often due to her inability to cope with relatively minor frustrations. Personal relationships can also fail due to her lack of adaptability, her moodiness and her general irritability.

- Affected adults suffer a general lack of self-esteem. Their whole life seems to be one long failure – both at home and at work. Very little seems to work out successfully for them, and they become used to accepting failure as the norm for them.

- They may suffer symptoms of anxiety and/or depression as a result of their low self-esteem.

- According to one American study, ADD sufferers were twice as likely to be involved with drug abuse, and drug-plus-alcohol abuse than a control group. An unhappy way to compensate for an unhappy life?

- Adults with ADD tend not to show the typical hyperactivity seen in children. Instead, their most frequently identified symptom is altered moods.

It is important to remember, however, that adults may be suffering from one of a number of psychiatric illnesses, some of which have similar symptoms to ADD. Skilled psychiatric help is needed to unravel these conditions.

Assessing ADD in adults

A complete medical history must be taken before any definite diagnosis is made. As with children, other physical and mental causes of behaviour-patterns must first be excluded. An important part of this exercise involves looking back at the person's behaviour as a child. ADD does not suddenly occur in adult life, but is a continuation (albeit in a modified form) of behaviour-patterns seen in childhood.

So if a person has a history of school failure and expulsion, with frequent changes of school, followed by similar failures at work, this will lend credence to a diagnosis of ADD in later life.

If there is a family history of problematic behaviour in childhood, this is also significant. This appears to be of greater significance if the affected members of the family are male.

A complete physical examination is carried out, along with any necessary associated blood-tests, X-rays or any other tests thought to be necessary, in order to exclude other medical conditions.

If it is possible, diagnosis can be helped when an observer, not immediately associated with either the person's home or work life, watches and records behaviour-patterns over a day or two; this provides useful objective evidence.

The final stages of diagnosis include psychological tests measuring abilities to understand and to live within the generally accepted social standards. The Brown AD/HD Scales are often used in this assessment (they can be used from the age of 12 upwards). A broad range of behaviour-patterns can be identified by these scales, such as:

- ways of activating and organizing work;
- abilities to sustain attention and effort;
- strategies for managing interference.

These tests can only be obtained and used by a qualified psychologist.

What can be done?

But what (it has been asked) is the point of identifying ADD in adults? After all, they have lived with the condition all their lives (if the diagnosis is correct), and have managed to struggle along so far. And what can be done to help at this late stage anyway?

Although it is understandable, it is a pity that this negative attitude persists. Much can be done, with an organized treatment plan, which includes:

- explaining the condition to sufferers, family and friends;
- suggesting educational and employment strategies;
- counselling by professionals on how best to manage the symptoms of the disorder;
- possibly taking some medication.

Some sufferers are profoundly relieved to be told that their negative feelings and attitudes are due to a known disorder – and, best of all, that something can be done, to improve their life.

1 Knowing about the condition

Knowing something about ADD is the first step along the way. Often sufferers will say, 'Oh, yes. That is just what happens'; or 'That is exactly how it feels'. Family and friends, too, will benefit from information on ADD. They will be more sympathetic to the sufferer's problems and, if asked for support and help, will offer them more willingly.

Joining an association concerned with ADD offers contact with other people also affected by the disorder. The literature available from such organizations will be of interest not only to sufferers but also to people closely in contact with them.

2 Education and employment

A sufferer's education may well have been upset by behavioural difficulties during childhood, so that the individual is not working to his, or her, full intellectual potential. Perhaps some new area of study, or some new hobby, can be started? Or some form of strenuous exercise begun? (Exercise will also serve as a useful outlet for hyperactivity, if this is factor, and also offers a chance to give vent to feelings of irritability or moodiness in a structured way.)

Joining a club or organization where the sufferer can meet people with similar interests will not only stimulate him intellectually, but also improve his self-esteem when successes occur.

Employment can be a worrying problem for ADD sufferers. A sympathetic careers officer or employment advisor could perhaps help with suitable employment ideas?

3 Counselling

All the above aspects can be helped along by a suitably qualified counsellor or coach. This person must understand fully the difficulties under which the adult with ADD labours, and must be able to suggest techniques which can help overcome the worst of the problems. It is best that this person should be outside the immediate family circle. Too close an involvement on a daily basis can be counterproductive.

A few of the techniques that can be helpful are:

- Use memos, diaries, lists and other personal devices to help with the disorganization aspects of ADD. Many people find a diary a necessity in organizing their social and working life – and this can work extremely well if you have the added problems of ADD, as long as you're not constantly losing it!
- Another way of avoiding disorganization is to establish a regular daily routine. Having a commitment to a regular job is of great value in this respect. But if this is not possible, it can help if you set certain tasks to be done at certain times.
- Breaking down larger tasks into smaller ones is also valuable. It is so much more satisfying to see just one tidy flower-bed, than attempting to tidy the whole garden. Prioritizing tasks is helpful, too. Get to grips with the most important, and finish these – even if it means that the less important ones are left undone.
- Do not be afraid to walk away from a difficult situation. If the temperature seems to be rising unhelpfully in a given situation, and you might fly off the handle, the best possible option is to walk away.
- Laugh with others at the problems associated with ADD – forgetfulness, disorganization or moodiness. Until such symptoms can be overcome, it is better to accept them and treat them with humour.

80

- Becoming enthusiastic and knowledgeable about just one aspect of life can raise self-esteem – whether it's gardening, martial arts, book-binding, woodwork, or whatever.

4 *Medication*

Medication must be taken with care, and only on medical advice. The different types of medication available are discussed in Chapter 8. It is also vitally important that the effects of any medication are monitored regularly.

Summary

Each adult diagnosed as having ADD will have their own specific problems – some symptoms being more prominent than others in each individual. A selection of the above techniques must be tailored to fit each individual. Perseverance will be necessary, but the rewards are great.

In short:

- ADD can be present in adults;
- signs and symptoms can be somewhat different from those seen in children;
- assessment must be complete and correct;
- a number of techniques are available to help.

Useful addresses

United Kingdom

The ADD/ADHD Family Support Group UK

1a High Street
Dilton Marsh
Westbury
Wilts BA13 4DL
01373 826045

Aims

- To promote awareness of the disorder to psychiatrists, psychologists, GPs, teachers, health visitors, social services.
- To support families of affected children and adults.
- To provide contact details for appropriate medical advice available.

Activities

- Seminars for health, education and welfare professionals.
- Regional meetings and workshops.
- Bi-monthly newsletter.
- Information leaflets available.

LADDER (National Learning and Attention Deficit Disorders Association)

PO Box 700
Wolverhamptom WV3 7YY
01902 336272

Aims

- To give advice and support to parents.
- To provide up-to-date information on ADD by regular attendance at international conferences.
- To offer information on doctors who have a special interest in ADD.

Activities

- Excellent quarterly newsletter (*Add-vice*).

- Publishes the LADDER Parent Guide to the 1993 Education Act & Code of Practice.

Hyperactive Children's Support Group

71 Whyke Lane
Chichester
West Sussex PO19 2LC
01903 725182

Aims

- To offer support and information over the telephone.
- To run local groups.

Activities

- Annual conference.
- Thrice-yearly journal.
- Promotion of research.

National Deaf Children's Society

15 Dufferin Street
London EC1Y 8PD
0171 251 0123

Aims

- To provide support through local groups.
- To offer specific advice to parents on health and education issues.

Activities

- Local group meetings.
- Quarterly magazine.
- Information leaflets.

RNIB (Royal National Institute for the Blind)

224 Great Portland Street
London W1N 6AA
0171 388 1266

Aims

- To offer information and advice for teachers and parents.
- To offer information on school-choices.
- To provide a parent support-group.

Activities

- Running of schools, colleges for visually impaired pupils.
- Rehabilitation centres.
- Information booklets and leaflets available.

MENCAP (for learning disabilities)

4 Swan Courtyard
Coventry Road
Birmingham B26 1BU
0121 707 7877

Aims

- To provide a forum on policy and practical issues.
- To offer support for families and individuals.
- To sponsor development projects and public education.
- To provide residential colleges for further education for 16–25 year-olds.
- To run a holiday service offering short-term respite care and holidays.

Activities

- Conferences, meetings locally, regionally and nationally.
- Newsletter – 10 issues per year.
- Information leaflets
- Series of publicity material available.

Learning and Assessment Centre

Health Centre
Lower Tanbridge Way
Worthing Road
Horsham
West Sussex RH12 1JB
01403 240002
This centre offers a service from educational psychologists and paediatricians for the diagnosis of ADD.

Contact a Family (CaF)

170 Tottenham Court Road
London W1P 0HA
Help line: 0171 383 3555

Contact a Family seeks to serve families who are caring for children with any type of disability or special need. The following services are available at local, regional and national levels in Britain:

- Advice and support to local parents' groups and to individual parents anywhere in the UK. Help is available from experienced staff at CaF's national office and other regional offices.
- A national help-line (number given above), answered by parent advisors. They will also answer written enquiries on any topic relating to children's disabilities and the help that is available.
- A Directory listing many disabilities found in children, together with the appropriate address and telephone where further help can be obtained. Regular six-monthly updates are available.
- A quarterly journal – *Share an Idea* – and fact-sheets on a variety of topics, such as special educational needs, welfare benefits, holidays, starting a parents' group.
- Publicity for the needs of families with a disabled child, and the presentation of the case for better services to central and local government and other public bodies.

United States

CHADD (Children with Attention Deficit Disorder)
Parent Support Group
499 NW 70th Avenue
Suite 308
Plantation
Florida 33317
This organization has around 300 chapters nationally and internationally, which provide support and information to parents and professionals. An excellent source for identifying local resources.

ADDA (Attention Deficit Disorder Association)
PO Box 972
Mentor
OH 44061

USEFUL ADDRESSES

Adult AH/HD Clinic
University of Massachusetts Medical Centre
Department of Psychiatry
55 Lake Avenue North
Worcester
MA 01655

Australia

Active Hyperkinetic Children's Association
PO Box 17
East Doncaster
Victoria 3109

Launceston Hyperactivity Association
C/-PO
Meander
Tasmania 7304

Queensland Hyperactivity Association
PO Box 204
Veronga
Queensland 4740

New Zealand

Auckland Hyperactivity Association Inc
PO Box 36-099
Northcote
Auckland

Waikato Hyperkinetic Children's Support Group
C/-10 McFarlane Street
Hamilton

USEFUL ADDRESSES

Canada

Canadian Institute of Child Health

17 York Street
Suite 202
Ottawa
Ontario K1N 5S7

Canadian Paediatric Society

Centre hospitalier universitaire de Sherbrooke
Sherbrooke
Quebec J1H 5N4

Further reading

There is a mass of specialized literature – articles and books – available on the subject of ADD. The following books will be of interest to parents who wish for a different view or presentation of ADD.

Alan Train, *AD/HD: How to deal with very difficult children*, Human Horizon Series, Souvenir Press.
This is an excellent book for parents and teachers wanting to know more about the educational needs of children with AD/HD.

Dr Christopher Green, *Understanding Attention Deficit Disorder – A Parent's Guide*, Vermilion.
This Australian book gives easy-to-understand (and amusing) information on ADD, together with many good ideas on treatment in a readable form.

Dr Sam Goldstein and Dr Michael Goldstein, *Hyperactivity – Why Won't My Child Pay Attention*, John Wiley.
This American book gives much valuable information on ADD, from both the psychology and medical angle, from writers who have much experience of the disorder.

Professor Eric Taylor, *Understanding Your Hyperactive Child*, Vermilion.
This book discusses hyperactivity in detail, with advice on how to handle the problem, by a British professor of psychiatry.

The Implementation of the Code of Practice for Children with Special Needs, HMSO Publications Centre, PO Box 276, London SW8 5DT (0171 873 9090).
Contains details of the legislation, briefly summarized in Chapter 7, concerning special-needs children.

Glossary

Amino acid
Smallest unit of protein.
Behaviour modification
Techniques used to change unacceptable behaviour.
Cerebral palsy
Primarily a disorder affecting movement, but sufferers may also have learning difficulties.
Cognition
Understanding.
Diabetes
Condition in which the body cannot control blood-sugars.
Dietician
Someone who specializes in all forms of food and nutrition.
Dysfunction
Not functioning normally.
Enzymes
Catalysts vital for the many chemical processes which take place in the body.
Epicanthus
Fold of skin on the inside of the eye.
Epilepsy
Condition in which convulsions occur.
Gene
Unit of inheritance.
Glue ear
Condition in which there is sticky fluid in the middle ear.
Health visitor
Nurse specializing in the care of families with young children.
Hormones
Substances produced by ductless, or 'endocrine', glands.
Identical twins
Two babies with the same genetic inheritance.
Non-identical twins
Twins with different genetic inheritance.

Paediatrician
Doctor who specializes in children's diseases.
Phenylketonuria
A condition caused by the absence of a specific enzyme.
Psychiatrist
Doctor specializing in mental illness.
Psychopathology
A psychological or mental illness.
Psychotropic drugs
Mind-altering drugs.
Psychologist
Specialist in the understanding of the mind, and in behaviour.
Respite care
Time out from the daily environment of caring for a sick or disabled person.
Retina
Part of the eye intimately connected with vision.
Single palmar crease
Having one crease only in the palm of the hand, instead of the usual two.
Special needs teaching
Special educational facilities for children with disabilities.
Statementing
The process of determining appropriate schooling for a child with special needs.
Syndrome
A collection of specific signs and symptoms which make up a named condition, e.g. Down's syndrome.
Thyroid gland
A ductless gland situated in the front of the neck.
Tic
A twitch, or involuntary movement of the body.
Tourette syndrome
A condition associated with involuntary tics.

Index

Index